LET'S MOVE ON

Paul Okalik Speaks Out

We've been pressing our national government to allow us to contribute to our sovereignty. We had a constant presence, and an historical use of the land in the Arctic. We're always used for the benefit of our country for asserting Canadian sovereignty over our traditional land, but at the same time we have to catch up to the rest of the world, support those communities and assert our presence in the modern world. And we're far from being there. It's nice to build icebreakers and those things, but where are they going to refuel? Where are they going to land their boats in our territory, if they have problems? It's still under development, but the facilities are not there. How are these decisions going to benefit our communities that are living there permanently? We see a total absence of investment in the people by the federal government. How will that allow us to grow and prosper like the rest of the country?

LET'S MOVE ON

Paul Okalik Speaks Out

Foreword by Honourable Paul Aarulaaq Quassa,
Premier of Nunavut

PAUL OKALIK

Historical Context by Louis McComber

Baraka
Books

MONTRÉAL

ISBN 978-177186-136-6 pbk; 978-1-77186-138-0 epub; 978-1-77186-139-7, pdf; 978-1-77186-140-3, mobi pocket

Front page map: Where We Live and Travel, courtesy of the Inuit Heritage Trust
Cover photo by Michel Albert
Back cover photo by Louis McComber
Book Design and Cover by Folio infographie
Editing by Robin Philpot
Proofreading Arielle Aaronson

Legal Deposit, 2nd quarter 2018

Bibliothèque et Archives nationales du Québec
Library and Archives Canada
Published by Baraka Books of Montreal
6977, rue Lacroix
Montréal, Québec H4E 2V4
Telephone: 514 808-8504
info@barakabooks.com

Printed and bound in Quebec

Trade Distribution & Returns
Canada and the United States
Independent Publishers Group
1-800-888-4741 (IPG1);
orders@ipgbook.com

We acknowledge the support from the Société de développement des entreprises culturelles (SODEC) and the Government of Quebec tax credit for book publishing administered by SODEC.

Société de développement des entreprises culturelles
Québec

Funded by the Government of Canada
Financé par le gouvernement du Canada

Canadä

Contents

Paul Okalik ice fishing at midnight (Photo: Brian Summers).

Acknowledgements

The interviews for this book were conducted when Paul Okalik was Minister of Justice in the Government of Nunavut. I am very thankful to Mr. Okalik for agreeing to work on a book project with me and, despite his busy schedule, granting me interviews. Le centre interuniversitaire d'études et de recherches autochtones (CIÉRA) of Université Laval provided financial support to the authors for this book project.

We are also grateful to Mélanie Gagnon who provided the maps of Nunavut for the book and Josh Worman who helped in the transcription and the editing of the manuscript. Special thanks to Michel Albert of Iqaluit who generously provided the front page photograph, to Ludger Müller-Wille and Bernd Gieseking for their photos, and to the Inuit Heritage Trust for allowing us to use the background map of Nunavut. Finally our publisher Baraka Books and its director Robin Philpot deserve our admiration for supporting this project all the way to its publication but also for all the inspiring books published by Baraka Books through the years.

Louis McComber
Sutton, February 2018

Acronyms

AIM	American Indian Movement
BRIA	Baffin Region Inuit Association
DEW	Distant Early Warning
GN	Government of Nunavut
GNWT	Government of the Northwest Territories
ITC	Inuit Tapirisat Canada (Now, Inuit Tapiriit Kanatami)
ITK	Inuit Tapiriit Kanatami (formerly, Inuit Tapirisat Canada)
DIAND	Department of Indian Affairs and Northern Development (Now Indigenous and Northern Affairs Canada (INAC))
NIC	Nunavut Implementation Commissioner
NLCA	Nunavut Land Claims Agreement
NTI	Nunavut Tunngavik Inc.
OIC	Office of the Interim Commissioner
QIA	Qikiqtani Inuit Association
RCAP	Royal Commission on Aboriginal Peoples
TFF	Territorial Financing Formula
UNDRIP	United Nations Declaration on the Rights of Indigenous Peoples

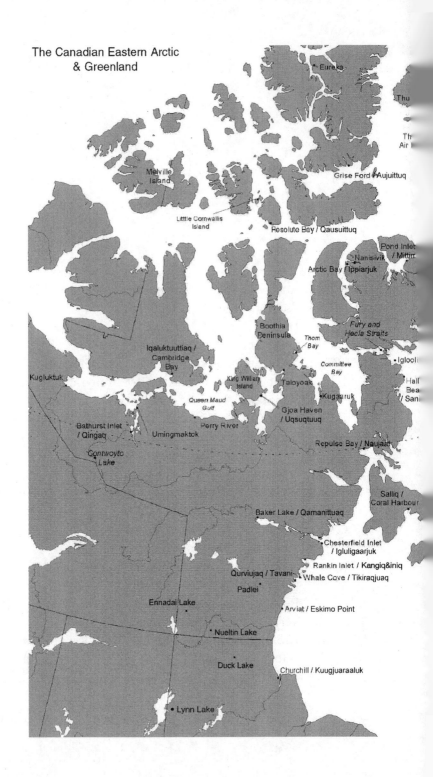

The Canadian Eastern Arctic & Greenland

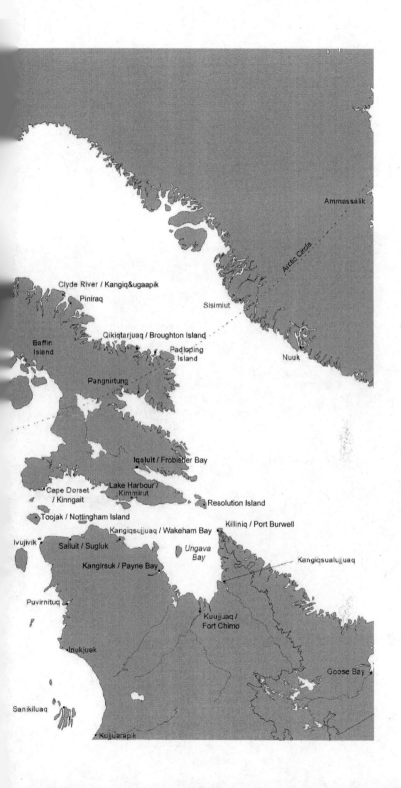

Inuit First

A Preface by Hon. Paul Aarulaaq Quassa, Premier of Nunavut

I remember very clearly the first time I met Paul Okalik in 1985. Tunngavik Federation of Nunavut was looking for regional negotiators and I applied, not knowing that Paul Okalik had also applied; I got interviewed and was hired right away.[1] I was hired as the South Baffin negotiator, as I was living in Iqaluit at the time. Paul Okalik applied while he was working at Nanisivik mine.[2] So he was hired as the North Baffin negotiator and I was hired as the South Baffin negotiator. The funny part is that I was originally from North Baffin, and Paul Okalik was originally from South Baffin. That is how we started working together.

The first time I met him is when he came down to Iqaluit and from there we flew to Sanikiluaq in the Hudson Bay to get trained and orientated. At first I thought that he was a fairly young man for the job. He is a lot younger than me.

On our way to Sanikiluaq, we had to overnight in Kuujjuarapik that was called Great Whale River then. We got stuck there because of the weather and as young people would do, we just hung out at the local bar, where we had a good time. Both of us were staying at the same hotel and we had a little fight that evening coming back to our rooms! The next day, Paul Sammurtok, who was our boss, found out that we had had a little fight and immediately fired us. Both of us! About a week after we were hired, he fired us! Me and Paul Okalik. "You're fired!" he told each of us. We didn't know what to do. We got rehired the very next day. That is how our very first week as Tunngavik Federation of Nunavut negotiators started!

Over the years, Paul and I were on the Nunavut Tunngavik negotiating team until 1990. I became Chief Negotiator from 1988 to 1993, and when the Government of Nunavut was created in 1999, Paul Okalik became the Premier. I was the President of Nunavut Tunngavik Inc. then. It worked out well. We know each other very well. Both of us were very much pro land claims. With me being at NTI and Paul Okalik in government, it worked very well. He knew what to do as Premier. Again, we still worked together when I became the Minister of Education in the Government of Nunavut and he was the Minister of Justice. Unfortunately he didn't get re-elected in 2017, but we are still in touch.

As the first Premier of Nunavut, he made sure the vision of Nunavut was kept well alive in the newly created territory. Our Inuit language was already a very strong component of the emerging Government of Nunavut. He created a new ministry very much centred on Inuit culture, the Department of Culture, Language, Elders and Youth. That was very much in line with what we envisioned for the Government of Nunavut, namely a government that truly respects the Inuit's language and culture. He kept that mission alive right from the start. I believe that we have the same goal. We want a government that truly respects our language and culture, which is something my government and I will strengthen even more. It takes a good many years to hold the government to what we envisioned when we were negotiators.

I want to see a government that is very strong in Inuit language. I want to make it mandatory for government employees to speak Inuktut.* Non-Inuit employees have to learn Inuktut. That was the vision we had when we negotiated the Government of Nunavut under our land claims agreement. Our government should understand and speak Inuktut and I'll make sure that it does. With Paul Okalik, it was always Inuit first. That has always been our number one priority. Even if this government is a public government, 85 percent of our population is Inuit. Recognizing that fact should be a priority among our territorial policies.

Of course when the Government of Nunavut was first created in 1999, it reflected the previous Northwest

---

* Inuktuk is a term that includes different dialects of the Inuit language all across the Arctic, such as Inuktitut and Inuinnaqtun, which are official languages in Nunavut.

Territories southern ways of thinking. It was a very Anglo kind of thinking in the way they delivered their programs. Very English.

I always envied Quebec, because with their Bill 101 or Charter of the French Language it made them so strong in making sure that their language is always the number one priority of their government. You don't see a situation like that anywhere else in other parts of Canada. Just in Nunavut and Quebec. In any other parts of the jurisdictions in Canada other than Nunavut, the indigenous populations are very small and are constantly fighting for their culture and language. Now in Nunavut we live it. It is just there.

Paul Okalik is very pro-Inuit culture and very much pro-language. I am very happy that when he first became Premier, that was in essence what he wanted to accomplish. But it will take years before we can completely reach our goals.

I'm so happy now as Premier of Nunavut to be part of that journey. The Inuit out there have so many expectations. Paul Okalik started the whole process and I am going to be part of the continuity. Hopefully we will succeed in meeting some of the expectations that Inuit had when we signed the Nunavut Land Claims Agreement.

Hon. Paul Aarulaaq Quassa
Premier of Nunavut
December 2017

I Was Young, Foolish, and Full of Energy!

A year or two before I was born, my family relocated from a camp called Idlungajung, which is southwest of Pangnirtung, in Cumberland Sound. That's where my late grandmother and grandfather, along with my great-grandfather Angmarlik, had established their camp.[1] My only living grandparent at the time was my grandmother Qatsuk. She was my mother's mother. My mother was the oldest of the children in her family. My father was Auyaluk. He had been adopted, which is why there are no really strong stories from my father's side, unfortunately.

My primary storyteller was my mother. I was lucky—I learned a lot about my family from my mother's side, and my late grandmother, Qatsuk. My great-grandmother was alive when I was born, but I have no living memory of her. She was the matriarch of the family. Her name was Asivak. I am told she was very strong. Her husband was Angmarlik, who was the whaling captain in Kekerten*. The women in the community were very

* Kekerten, both a harbour and an island at the mouth of Kingnaite Fjord in Cumberland Sound, is part of a group of islands whalers often

Angmarlik distributing biscuits to Inuit who unloaded Hudson's Bay Company supplies from R.M.S. NASCOPIE [From left to right: Angmarlik, Ipeelie Kilabuk, Isiasie Angmarlik (boy with the hood), Kitturiaq (man with the hood), Pauloosie Angmarlik (man in the far back in front of the tools), Inoosiq Nashalik (younger man second from right), Sakey Evic (boy not wearing his hood being given a biscuit) and Atagoyuk (man on the far right).] (George Hunter, NFB, LAC, PA-166458)

strong. My late mother told me stories about what they had to do. My father had health issues. My mother had to work hard to provide support for the family. We had some challenging times, I must say. My mother was our primary caregiver, and she raised us well.

My first memories are of living with my family in a matchbox house, one of the first houses that were con-

_____

called "the Kekertens"—Kikistan Islands on current maps. Kekerten was one of the most important whaling sites during most of the over-wintering whaling period.

Aasivak Evic, wife of Angmarlik and grandmother of the Evic family, is drying "kamiks" in front of her tent. Mount Duval is visible in the background in August 1946. (George Hunter, NFB, LAC, PA-166445)

structed in the North for Inuit families. They were one-room units. For the bathroom, there was a little 'honey bucket' near the porch. There was an oil-burning stove for heat. No running water; very basic. It was like living in a cabin today. There was no phone, no radio or TV. It was all family, all in Inuktitut. My closest sibling was my sister Looee. She was a couple of years older than me. I also remember my brothers Norman and Joelle. The other siblings had moved on. They got married; they were living their own lives, and having kids. Not long after, we moved to a bigger unit, one with two bedrooms. I was probably three or four, the youngest of the family.

Not long before I was born, my great-grandmother converted from Siina, the traditional shamanic religion—to the Anglican religion.[2] I'm told that when she converted, she made a huge *amauti* of caribou skin, and put it in the ocean to apologize to Siina for converting to Christianity. I missed that era, but the stories were passed on to me. My own family, my mother and grandmother in particular, were quite religious. For myself, I was more or less regressing at times, because I was young, foolish, and full of energy! I thought there were other things to do besides religion. As young people, we were facing more traumatic times. We found ourselves at a turning point: trying to adjust to a community, while trying to follow some of the traditional practices. It was a challenging time. We were living in an era where our parents never attended school. We were living our own lives, separate from our parents. It was a completely different experience.

I watched the kids as they walked to school when I was three or four. I remember getting bored during the day. I begged my mother Annie to bring me to school. I was the youngest, my mother's baby. I wanted to have other kids to play with. Finally, my mother couldn't take it any more, and she convinced the school teacher to take me in a year early. How could I know how bad it was at school? It wasn't long before she had to beg me to wake up in the morning to go to school. It was a traumatic time. They insisted that you only speak English in the school. Even to go to the washroom, you had to ask in English. If you didn't know how, then you couldn't go. There were some very unfortunate experiences for me. My mom suffered through most of it. We had no running water, and she had to wash my clothes. It was not a good time for me, and it was embarrassing.

I don't have a lot of memories from school. What I do remember most are the breaks, the summer months, when we would go camping as a family. We would go to our traditional camps, and learn about our history, from my

Cumberland Sound from the top of Mount Duval overlooking the hamlet of Pangnirtung on Baffin Island where Paul Okalik was born. (Photo: Louis McComber)

mother. Those are the best memories I have, of growing up. I still live through those memories today. I caught my first fish—I must have been six. I caught my first seal and my first caribou when I was eight.

I remember going to our traditional caribou hunting grounds. It was quite a ways from Pangnirtung. You had to cross Cumberland Sound and go into Nettilling Fjord. Netsiliariaq; it's where you go towards Nettilling Lake.[3] We went by boat and on foot. It was a lot of work: you had to carry the caribou on your back, and there were places where you had to portage. It was lots of work, but it gave me good memories. We worked as a family unit; we were hunting caribou to feed the family. We didn't have CBs or radios, and when it was really dangerous, because of the currents, for example, we went along with other families. I have some really good memories of catching my first caribou, learning how to skin a caribou, and then seal. It was exciting. The caribou were abundant then. That's where my ties are. I have cravings for caribou, even today! That's how I grew up, that was our primary diet, along with fish and *maqtaaq*, a layer of skin and fat of the beluga whale. When I was young there was a quota on beluga hunting. I never hunted it, but I really loved the *maqtaaq*. I still crave it and can't get enough of it. It's still my favourite food.

What I remember the most are stories that my mother passed on about how to respect and treat the environment. She would often scold me for being messy. She said we shouldn't leave anything behind in caribou country. She taught me to respect the land, to treat it properly, and to treat the remains properly. I once threw a caribou bone on the shoreline. My mother said, "Caribou does not belong in the ocean. It belongs on the land. You do not throw caribou remains in the ocean!" And vice-versa for the seal. These are things that I remember and respect to this day. That's how we should treat our environment, with respect and understanding for the species that we still depend on.

Fur prices were very good for seal. Another memory I have is my father working for a salary, but relying on the fur trade for additional income. He was a water truck driver in Pangnirtung. He used to arrange his vacation in the summer months so that we could vacation as a family. We didn't do a lot of hunting in the winter, because we were in school and my father was working. The odd time, we would go caribou or seal hunting in the winter.

Paul Okalik chatting with Jean Béliveau when the Montreal Canadien hockey star visited Pangnirtung in mid 1970's. (Photo: Paul Okalik)

I do remember listening to the Montreal Canadiens on the radio, when I first started paying attention to the outside world. I didn't care about anything else. The teacher tried to show us videos of the Toronto Maple Leafs! I didn't care about the Toronto Maple Leafs—I was interested in my Montreal Canadiens. Pete Mahovlich was my player.[4] I didn't really care about the rest!

Where I grew up, there was no arena, no pond, and no lake. We didn't have any skates or equipment, either. We just had hockey sticks and the odd puck now and again. We played a lot of street hockey, every night in the winter, and floor hockey in the gym, later on, when I was a little older. If the creek was frozen properly, we could skate on it. But I didn't learn how to skate very well.

For the members of my extended family who didn't have jobs, their lives were focused on hunting seals and selling the skins. I shot my first seal when I was eight years old. The custom was to give your first skin to your *arnaliaq*, your godmother. But I didn't have one. My godmother was a nurse, who had moved on. She was the nurse who helped my mother, who delivered me. Aniasuutiqutah was her name: "Tall nurse." Since I didn't have anyone to give it to, I said, "I'll sell it to the Hudson's Bay Company." My mother wanted to keep it. But I said, "I don't have *arnaliaq*, so too bad." My father said, "Okay, go ahead!" So my first income was from a sealskin. That got me addicted and hooked. In the summer, I spent quite a bit of time seal hunting. I remember going out alone, at the age of sixteen, in July, in a boat by myself, hunting seals. If it was a harp seal, we wouldn't keep the meat, we'd dispose of it. The fur prices were better for harp seals. We would keep ring seal meat for the family.

I don't have a lot of memories about school in Pangnirtung. I remember only some of the teachers. Some were mean. They would hit us. One teacher broke her ruler on me. Those things happened. I guess I was pretty young and foolish. That was their way of punishing us. Other ones were very good. But I don't remember a lot. I have more memories about grade seven and grade eight. But I didn't focus too hard on my education. I didn't understand what good it would do me. Looking at my environment, there weren't a lot of opportunities at the time. My goal was to become a hockey player for the Montreal Canadiens, but we had no arena and I couldn't skate! I was pretty good at floor hockey, though. I didn't see the point in what we were learning. I had never seen an Inuk attending university or college. We didn't care too much about schooling; that was just how it was. We were just trying to adjust to a new environment. We had other distractions. Our parents had never lived through our experience, so they couldn't relate to us or assist us in our schoolwork. My late mother said, "Just focus on school, and get an education. I won't be around forever, and I want you to have the best job possible, and a secure future." She was wise that way, she always looked ahead. She was looking after our well-being. At the time, I never really listened.

I had another experience that wasn't very good for me. I was quite young, just becoming a teenager. My late brother Norman, who I looked up to very much, really was a good brother. He was quiet, and he really looked after me. He was in the cadets, doing his thing, travelling to jamborees now and again. I guess he had been exposed to drugs, to marijuana. He apparently had broken into the hamlet office and took some money, but nobody caught him. A number of months later, he felt bad, and he turned himself in to the police, explaining what he did. He wasn't treated very well. He was sentenced to jail and fined. He did his time, but when it came time to pay his fine he didn't have the money. He couldn't take it. He didn't want to go back to jail. I could see it. He wasn't all there, he had a heavy burden. He stayed in bed most days. It was hard to watch. I was young; I didn't know what to do. I was coming home from school one day, and my family was all home. My mother came to me and said, "You won't see your brother again." I said, "What?" "Your brother Norman. He shot himself this morning." That was my turning point. It was very traumatic. I became very angry and distraught. How could they treat him like that, after he tried to cooperate? I was very bitter and angry. I didn't care any more. I was thirteen, and Norman was eighteen. It was a challenging time for our family. There hadn't been very many suicides in Pangnirtung.

My late father had mental issues. This ate him up, and he had to be shipped out for treatment. My mother pretty much carried the family, during that time. I was angry and twisted. It was really difficult. Whenever things came up, like arguments with other kids, they would say things like, "You're crazy like your father, who had to be shipped out!" That kind of stuff hurts. It made me even angrier. It was hard for my family. It made me very bitter towards the law. I had no respect for the police and authority at that time. Our teachers asked, "What do you want to do?" I replied, "I want to become a lawyer." I had never seen an Inuk lawyer, let alone an Inuk working in the court system. It was foreign to us. But I was dreaming up opportunities to try and help out.

I got into trouble. I became dysfunctional, questioning authority. I didn't really care for anything, at that point. I had gone to cadet camps a few times outside the territory. But I didn't really care for school too much. We just had cadets, school, then after-school floor hockey.

I had one good teacher who focused me a bit towards school. His name was Mike Medwig. He was the one who helped me focus on my learning. I had struggled with reading quite a bit. He was very helpful. There was only one teacher, Mike Gardener, who spoke Inuktitut.[5] The rest were all focused on teaching us English. I had one good year in grade eight. But I struggled in math in grade nine, then totally lost interest and dropped out, despite my mother's pleadings to stay in school. I left school, and I spent a year making trouble, just being a teenager.

I drank, and I experimented with drugs. But drinking was my drug of choice. Even though it was a dry community, we made home brew and other things that were mind-altering. I was being a rebel, and hanging out with my cousins. I would go hunting the odd time in the summer. But I never really learned how to hunt in the winter. I went on the odd fishing trip in the spring.

I went back to adult education in Pangnirtung to try being in school again. Mary Ellen Thomas was the adult educator then.[6] The following year, in 1981-82, I was finally accepted here in Iqaluit for grade ten. I was admitted in the fall, and stayed at the Ukivik residence. I was more focused on drinking and partying at the time. I didn't last six months. I did okay at school, but I was kicked out of the residence by February of 1982. I'm not proud of it, but that's how it was at the time. I was going through some challenges in my personal life. From there, I got more heavily into drinking and partying; I partied and got into trouble. I ended up in jail, in April of that year. There was no Young Offenders Act at the time, so I did adult time, for breaking and entering.[7]

I was pretty lost in those days. I didn't know what to do with my life. I was doing okay at school, but my problem was after school. I was active at the Iqaluit bar, 'The Zoo.' My oldest brother Joelle was working there. He was seven years older than me. He was feeling a lot of remorse about the death of our late brother. He was very protective of me; he spoiled me. He even gave me his I.D. to get in the bar.

After a while, I decided that the jail thing wasn't working out so well. I did some more upgrading and got myself accepted into college at Fort Smith in the fall of 1982, for an introduction to welding program. It was something to do! My mother was very supportive. I stayed in Fort Smith until the spring. After that, I managed to get a job up in Nanisivik Mine, as a welding apprentice.[8] I lived and worked there until February of 1985.

Pangnirtung Fiord at low tide looking northeast, July 2007
(Photo: Bernd Gieseking).

CHAPTER 2

I Was Thinking About Tomorrow

My late brother Norman had worked at the Nanisivik mine as well, so I was following in his footsteps. My mother was happy; at least I was working, putting some of my education to use. She was very proud of me. But I was still partying heavily. My job was a way of supporting my drinking habit, but it kept me out of trouble.

I was an apprentice welder at the time. I found it rather mundane, because I had an active mind. I switched over and started working as an apprentice mechanic there. I got into repairing things, and did that for maybe half a year. They would let me drive big equipment now and again, to help out around the garage, even though I had no driving permit. It was fun. It was a good experience, but very dirty. Lots of oil and mud. You had to crawl under heavy equipment to fix them. I worked in Nanisivik for almost two years, until January or February of 1985. The winters were very hard; it was so dark, 24/7, for two months. Where I grew up, there was at least some daylight. My body couldn't take the darkness. During the winter months, I had to take a break and travel south. Even there, I was a bit of a troublemaker.

In the winter, I was on night shift at the garage. Once, I was five minutes early for the bus to take me to my shift, but it never came. So I just went home for the night. The following day, my supervisor came and asked me why I missed my shift. I told him that I couldn't get to work, because there was no bus. So he explained that to the superintendent, and the superintendent asked me to sign a document saying I was AWOL.[1] I said, "No, I'm not gonna sign. I was not provided with the required transportation and I couldn't get to work." It wasn't my fault. And that's how we left it. I knew my rights. We didn't have a union.

I had some time on my hands, so I followed the news, and since I was still struggling with reading, I had to upgrade to prepare myself for an apprenticeship. My training required me to read, but I was still struggling. I got into reading a bit more, ordering stuff, learning how to read a bit more; it was self-development. That was my thing, even though I was still partying on the side. It was a fun time, I must say. I was making money, partying, being young.

In 1985, Nunavut was making the news. There was a position open for a regional research negotiator at the Tungavik Federation, the Nunavut land claims organization. I saw the ad, and thought, Hmm, this looks challenging. I applied and sent in my résumé. Up to that point, I hadn't been too involved in politics. But I was curious, and I followed anything that had to do with the law. I was always on the lookout for something more stimulating, even though I was still quite angry, given my family's history with the law. I had participated in student politics in the past, in grade eight, my favourite academic year. In high school, I was quite good in social studies and politics.

I struggled mightily in math. My late mother was quite active in Pauktuutit, the national Inuit women's association. She travelled quite a bit. She was firm, straight; she was good at guiding me by example. She never talked a lot about politics with me, but she knew how to be effective.

By chance, I got an interview for the job, over the phone. I was still apprenticing at Nanisivik. Johnny Illupalik interviewed me. He was the Baffin representative at the Baffin Region Inuit Association (BRIA).[2] He was on the executive. He was doing most of the talking. I learned that he was the main one that got me hired. He had to argue with the others, who thought I was too young. I was only twenty years old at the time; this was February of 1985. I got hired, and from that point on, there was a lot of learning! I had to move to Frobisher Bay.[3] I was hired by the Baffin Region Inuit Association to work for the Tunngavik Federation of Nunavut as a North Baffin researcher and negotiator. I got hired on with Paul Quassa. We started on the same day, February 5, 1985. He was the negotiator for South Baffin, and I was the North Baffin negotiator. He was originally from Igloolik in North Baffin, and I was from Pangnirtung, in South Baffin! It was a fun time. We were learning a lot together. It got me into reading a lot more. There was no training to be a land claims researcher and negotiator. We learned on the job. We got a bit of an orientation, telling us what the situation was; there were only about five agreements signed at the time, pretty much. We did our learning on the job. We attended board meetings.

In terms of my own interests, I worked a lot with wildlife. I went to meetings to consult, and to get direction. I met with a lot of people. I understood a lot more about challenges throughout the territory. It got me grounded.

My mother wasn't happy. Here I was, doing so well up North, and moving to a different job. She would have liked me to stay with one job. She pleaded with me. But I wanted something more challenging. Once she understood what I was trying to do, she was very supportive of my efforts.

We were negotiating the wildlife agreement in principle. The water agreement and the land use planning agreement in principle had already been negotiated. The rest were still outstanding articles. We still needed to negotiate environmental protection, finalize wildlife provisions, and work on how land would be selected, how much land would be negotiated. Also, who would benefit from the land claims agreement? And from the financial compensation? Those things had not been worked out. Not a lot had been finalized up to that point. Nunavut was still a dream at the time, something we talked about, but we couldn't quite believe we would get there some day.

We participated in the negotiation meetings. There were one-week monthly sessions that we prepared for, with the federal and territorial government of the day. We were back and forth between Ottawa and the North. We had sessions in Yellowknife, Kugluktuk, Pangnirtung, Iqaluit. The feds needed some expertise and bureaucracy, and board meetings in between. We were really aware of the political climate of the day. Sometimes we had to defend what we had already reached an agreement on. I would be the 'detail guy.' If there was a question, I was there to pinpoint the subsection.

I always knew that the land claims negotiations would end up in a land transaction. My primary focus was to look after what was left, what lands we would not select; what was not up for negotiation—protecting our right to hunt, to help regulate that environment. I grew up knowing the sensitivity of our environment, making sure it would be protected. That was my biggest focus. I knew at the end of the day, we were going to lose some of that land. We had to make sure that there was enough protection there for future generations. Even though it's not your land, *per se*, at least you have a say over it. Our negotiating process was generally supported by our communities, at the time. But we had to be aware that once that agreement was signed, we would have to live with it. We wouldn't get another kick at the can. We had to make sure it was done properly. That was a big challenge, trying to find the balance. I wasn't focused on the present; I was thinking about tomorrow.

There were some good people I worked with who gave me guidance. The first lawyer I was exposed to was David Bennett.[4] He was our young lawyer. He had been involved in the Inuvialuit land claims agreement that were negotiated by Simon Reisman, who represented Canada in the AutoPact, in the free trade agreement.[5] He had that type of negotiating skill. We knew the magnitude of our discussions, and how it was important for future generations. We got along quite well. He pushed me to learn more about the laws, and he told me that I could become a lawyer, if I wanted to. He was my inspiration.

There was also an economist by the name of Fred Weihs. I did a lot of research work with him on programs. He inspired me to do more, to value my work. So I was exposed to some very good people who cared about the land claims, and about the work we did. It gave me more focus.

We were negotiating, arguing about what was going to be in the subsections—the wording of the legal text. You had to have lawyers around all the time, to negotiate the wording. It exposed me to that type of work. Some of the lawyers weren't as smart as me. That gave me the confidence to possibly explore law school, as an avenue.

I worried a lot about how we were going to protect the rights of the Inuit in the long run. I wasn't concerned with how much land we'd get, at the end of the day. It's there, regardless of who wants it, as long as we can use it to our advantage. We'll always use it; we'll always find ways to benefit from it.

I worked well with the Makivik people.[6] They were very helpful, and they taught us about their experience. For example, they told us to make sure that certain boards and agencies "have more teeth," and not just be advisory bodies. I worked mostly with their research staff, but now and again I would get the chance to chat with Charlie Watt, who remains a very good friend to this day.[7]

We didn't have a lot of connections with Greenland. We were more focused on Canada at the time, in our discussions. Inuvialuit had signed their land claims agreement in 1984,[8] mostly because of the impacts of oil exploration in their region.

At times, I found the job challenging. I was pretty stubborn, always wanting more. I struggled with the negotiating team on some basic issues: look at eligibility and enrolment, for example. Who will be a beneficiary, in the land claims agreement? Up to that point, it was determined on the amount of blood you might have. I had to work to convince the rest of the crew. Let's let the Inuit decide, for example. I had to argue with them, to present that as an option. And when we presented it to the other side, they had no issue with it. So, we were able to get an agreement fairly quickly. As a young man, things like that were difficult. I wanted more for our beneficiaries in the future.

I took some time off here and there, to relieve myself of the stress. It was challenging.

I turned to drinking quite a bit near the end, due to stress. I also lost my dad in 1986 and my mom in 1989. I wasn't all there. I realized that I might need help. I tried going back to school, to the University of Carleton in Ottawa, to try and find a focus. But that didn't work. I took myself out of school, to work on my life. And in 1991, I found out I was going to be a dad. I thought, "I need to clean up my life." I left work, moved on, went home to Pangnirtung to focus on my life, planning to go back to school in the fall of 1991 to study law. The agreement in principle was reached in 1990, so the details were pretty much settled. It was a quite a struggle. My late grandmother Qatsuk was still around. I spent a lot of time looking after her. My oldest sister, my late sister Idah, was very good at reinforcing what I should do. They were very supportive. At one point, in Ottawa, I was suicidal with the amount of alcohol in me, and my sister saved me.

When I went to my grandmother and told her I was going to seek treatment for my alcoholism, she was very proud. She said, "If only your mother was here, to hear you say that. She'd be very happy." My sister was strong and loving, and she pushed me along positively. I had some very good people looking after me. This was my half-sister. When my mother passed on, she became my mother, pretty much. She helped me a lot.

I was accepted at Carleton University that fall. My sister Looee took me in and gave me support. I had become a father in June of that year, on the 26th. It was an adjustment, but it was a very positive development. My daughter's mother was living in Ottawa. That gave me a chance to spend time with my child, while I went to school. It was very good. My first year was a challenge. Just writing was a struggle, not to mention producing papers. I had friends and family to help me. After the first year, I developed more confidence.

Student assistance didn't pay very well. Nunavut Tunngavik Inc. helped me, in terms of summer work. I worked for them during the year whenever I could. I got involved in the ratification tour, since I was good at explaining the details of the agreement. When it was finalized, I kept working on the implementation side. I kept in touch with my colleagues.

Paul Okalik with his three sisters from l. to r., Jeannie, the late Idah (eldest sister), and Looee.

CHAPTER 3

My Studies Made Me
a Proud Inuk

I started my first year at Carleton in the fall of 1991. I knew Ottawa well as I had lived there for quite a while when we were finalizing the Nunavut Land Claims Agreements. I had strong ties to Nunavut Tunngavik Inc. I went into political science and Canadian studies. The first year was a struggle financially, and I was supporting my first child, as well. It was a challenge, trying to stay in balance. My sister Looee really saved me, during my first year. I realized that I had an interest in the law, that I could probably become a lawyer. I adjusted my lifestyle. When my first child was on the way, I became determined to make a change in my life. I was very grateful for the support I received from my family and friends. It made it easier for me to move on, and become more productive.

It was a big adjustment. Each lecture class in first year had about five hundred students. I had never been studying in that kind of environment before. You have to work with other students. The teaching assistants were helpful too. In first year, I had one professor who really challenged me, named George Rosemé. He was tough, but he pushed us to become better. With my keen interest to learn more, I would go and discuss with the teachers. It was good, it made me more focused. I was the only Inuk in my classes, and that made me feel like I was alone. At the same time, I was determined to succeed. I knew that if I could succeed, others could follow.

The funding I got was never sufficient to cover my costs in school and support my family. I had to work, to make ends meet. At the tail end of my studies, I had a six-year period of study to succeed in law. Finishing up my second-last year, in the middle of my exams in April 1990, the financial assistance office sent me a letter, saying I was cut off from any more funding from my government, since I had spent so much time in the South. That made it even more challenging, to get the news in the middle of my exams. I had to scramble. Luckily, the Mississauga First Nation came up to the plate, and funded my last year. That was my best year. I got my money on time, for studying in my final year.

When I was elected to the Government of Nunavut, one of the first areas I focused on was to provide more support for post-secondary students. I increased that financial support, over the two terms I was in government. I did what I could to make sure that my government did more to help students survive while studying.

At the time, you were required to do two years of university before entering law school. I looked at the programs, and I thought, "I only have one more year to go, and I'll get one more degree, before I get my law degree." So I chose a three-year program, instead of wasting two years of study. I added one more year and got my degree in Political Science and Canadian Studies. I applied at the University of Ottawa law school, and luckily I was accepted in 1994. When I was accepted, in May of '94, I was running around like a little boy! I was so happy and excited. I couldn't wait for September!

My studies gave me more opportunities to learn in detail about how our system works, about our history, as Canadians. At the same time, a lot of the courses in Canadian Studies allow you to look at your own history. It allowed me to travel home, to interview my family, elderly members of my family, and learn more about myself.

It really helped me. I got stronger, as a person. My studies made me a proud Inuk. I learned about what we did, in our history, to get to where we are today. It felt really rewarding to write papers about such things.

My late sister told me a lot about our family history, about the hardships they faced. Also, how lucky we are, in some ways, with today's opportunities and conveniences. It was far more challenging back in the days. There are a lot of problems, with the things we're exposed to today, but we need to take advantage of the opportunities that present themselves to us.

One of the gifts that my family passed on to me is the ability to move on. To look at the challenges we have, today and tomorrow. I have no regrets about the Nunavut Land Claims Agreement, we did as much as we could. We managed to change policy, during our negotiations. Before our wildlife board, there had never been so much authority passed on, to a board, for example. Up to that point, there had been no policy for negotiating the offshore rights. We said that we wouldn't sign anything that didn't include the offshore rights. And we succeeded; we changed policy and included the offshore. We said we wouldn't sign anything without a territorial government, our own government.

And we changed the land mass in our country. Those things, I must say, were challenging; but we did it. Everyone talks about all the negative stuff, but look at all the challenges we were faced with. Look at some of the details in Article 2, for example. It contains terms that you've never seen before, that protect the land claims agreement and the rights that you have. I haven't seen them since. Those are special sections that we put in there, for our own protection, for future generations. We insisted on them, to make sure we had a secure future for our rights and benefits in the land claims agreement.

When I was at university, I was focused on trying to learn, and keeping my marks high enough to get by. I was busy trying to support my family while studying. It was a challenge, but a good challenge. It kept me busy, kept me focused on my own development. I tried to get back up North every summer. I missed only one summer, because I had to work, I was helping out on land claims issues. I did make it up every other summer, and visited with my children.

On the first day, we had orientation. They said, "Look. There were twelve students that applied for your spot. You should consider yourselves very lucky to be here. Use it, and learn while you're here." That gave me a boost. "Wow, I made it. I'm living the dream!"

The first term was a good challenge; it made me aware of what to focus on. At the same time, it woke me up! I realized that I had to focus more. I was there with other aboriginal students. We helped each other out when we could. We also learned from some very good professors, who knew how to teach and keep us focused. Some of the best ones helped me, taught me what to study for in law school. It pushes us to look for the details. For example, in law, they write judgments, and you're supposed to read it and learn it and explain what the outcome is, what that decision was arrived at. It forces you to study all the details, and think critically. I struggled in my first year, and just got by. After that, it became easier. It was a very good experience, it taught me a lot.

Up until then, I had been carrying a burden, the memory of my late brother. There was an excellent professor named David Paciocco who taught criminal law.[1] After one of his lectures I went to visit him, I explained the situation. He was very supportive of my experience. He explained to me that the law is not always fair, towards the Inuit people. He taught me a lot. It's not really the law; it's the way it's structured and applied that is not fair. It gave me a new focus that we should move on, and look for ways to avoid those experiences. We need to share our experiences, so it doesn't happen again. I was focused on learning the British justice system, so I could think about how we can adjust it to our own expectations. We have to think about ways to tinker with the system, to adapt it to some of our own practices. That's what I was focusing on: why are things this way, and not that way? It gave me more perspective on different areas of law, how they arrived at those laws, and why we're stuck with some of them. I couldn't change all those laws, but we could work on ways of making them work better. Common law principles come from judges, but they can be over-ridden by legislative laws, laws made by legislature. There's ways of improving those. But our laws, as Inuit, were unwritten. They were more like codes that you respected and followed, as a community, to survive.

You had to follow what was being taught, to keep your marks high enough in order to get by. The only real mention of Inuit in law in the program was in property class, where the federal government of 1939 was trying to offload Inuit responsibilities to Quebec.[2] Ottawa didn't want to pay for Inuit services. It was ruled that, under the British North America Act, that Eskimos were actually Indian, so the federal government had responsibility for the Inuit. From there, we were defined as Indians, under the Constitution. That was about it, in terms of Inuit being involved in courts at the time.

My studies of the British system gave me new tools, to look at policies, to look at our condition as Inuit in Canada. I also learned that we weren't alone, as I was opening up to the challenges of other aboriginal groups in Canada. I was also hanging out with the gay and lesbian community a lot more; we talked about minority rights, discrimination, they were very understanding of aboriginal issues. It was an awakening. I realized that we're not alone, and that we can do better. We can improve our condition, within the system of Canadian justice.

I looked at our history, and how we interacted. For all of the negative connotations that exist with the Crown, the monarchy, and Britain, they did what they could. They tried to protect aboriginal land from being sold off, to settlers of the day. That gave us at least some recognition, that we had special rights. I was pleased to learn about that. Somebody was trying to protect our well-being, even way back then. I struggled more with criminal law, where my family had some very bad experiences with the system. I lost focus because I was feeling a lot of anger. When I was studying the law and I saw how badly it was applied to my late brother, I felt that it was so unfair. That was a challenge. But in terms of property law, I learned about how the monarchy was trying to protect our rights, way back then. When you look south of the border, aboriginal groups didn't do so well. At least in Canada, we were being protected in some ways. Unfortunately, it's criminal law as a federal responsibility that impacts us the most, as Inuit. We had our own way of addressing these issues. It made us stronger, as a family unit. And the way the system is structured is contrary to how we were raised. We were raised to support each other, to find ways to make our unit stronger. The criminal justice system is very individualistic, and focuses on the crime, not the individual. It fractures our Inuit system. It's one area, as an Inuk, I found difficult to study. I'd rather stick to our own traditional system.

CHAPTER 4

We Had to Make the Government Work

We were about sixty students in my first year at the University of Ottawa law school. Some didn't make it past their first year and we didn't see them anymore. It was stressful. It was a challenge for everyone.

Every chance I got, I took Professor David Paciocco's classes, because he was very clear and right to the point.[1] In my first year, he was teaching criminal procedure. He was very understanding and I tried to keep in touch with him now and then. He's been appointed a court judge in Ontario, and he is still doing very good work. I'm very proud of him.

After completing my law school, I was pleased to attend my graduation. It was really special for me and my family. They understood how hard it had been for me to get there. It was nice to see them all there.

I came back to Iqaluit in July of 1997. My only challenge was trying to get home. I had been cut off from my student funding by the Northwest Territories student services. I had to write to the Minister to ask for a plane ticket to

Paul Okalik at his law school graduation at University
of Ottawa in 1997 with his two children, daughter Shasta
and son Jordan.

go back home. The federal Department of Indian Affairs
and Northern Development would not pay for my airfare
either. Luckily, student services agreed that they had cut
me off prematurely.

It was frustrating for post-secondary students; we
wouldn't always get our money on time to buy books and
food. Financially it was difficult. I lived off Cup-a-Soup all
through university.[2] To this day I can't eat them any more.
That kind of a sacrifice is worthwhile, because you work

so hard to get where you want to go. It made me a stronger person, even more determined to succeed.

I went back to Iqaluit after six years in Ottawa, but even while I was gone I had been back regularly, whenever I could. I stayed in touch with people. When I passed the bar exam, it was a really special time. I had worked so hard, made so many sacrifices. I was very proud to have my family here, to be able to celebrate with them. They were with me all the way.

Financial support for Inuit students is an ongoing challenge. I made a commitment when I was in government, to increase support for them, but also allow them to study here in Nunavut. The government of the day expanded the Nunavut Teacher Education Program (NTEP), to allow students to study in their home communities.[3] We introduced a nursing program, as well as the Akitsiraq law school at the Nunatta campus of the Nunavut Arctic College in Iqaluit, so that people could complete their post-secondary education in Nunavut.[4] When students have to go elsewhere, it's a lot more challenging. You need your family around for support.

When I was studying in Ottawa, I kept up with the news but the situation in Nunavut didn't preoccupy me that much. My number one goal was becoming a lawyer, the rest was secondary. But once I came back home, I followed Nunavut politics more closely.

I had to move on to one year of articling, on-the-job training. I only applied to Nunavut because I wanted to go home to practice. Luckily I was accepted to work as an articling student by Ann Crawford and I started working in Iqaluit.[5]

I had good support from Ann Crawford; she did civil, corporate, and family law. She assisted me in adjusting,

Paul Okalik was received at the Nunavut Bar in 1999. He is celebrating here with his daughter Shasta in his arms.

and learning about the files. She allowed me to article at Maliiganik Tukisiiniakvik, the Iqaluit legal aid clinic, and also at a corporate firm in Yellowknife, even though she needed my help in her office. She was good to me that way.

In the Northwest Territories, the jurisprudence and the court system was different from what I had studied in Ontario. I had to do my bar exam in Alberta, of all places. This was another challenge because my studies were in Ontario law, I was working under the Northwest Territories law, and my bar exam was under the Alberta law. I would never work in Alberta as a lawyer, but I still had to study their rules of court, their civil procedure. It was frustrating. It was a real burden on me. It took me six months longer than I would have liked to pass the exam and move on. Luckily, Ann was very understanding, and I had the help of one of her students, who helped me study.

In December of 1998, I was at the tail end of my studies, and thinking at the challenges of forming a new government in the Nunavut territory. I realized that there was a way I could be more useful than practicing law. When I was doing my articling, I realized that you couldn't help as many people as you want. To access your services, people have to be able to pay you. I figured that I could help more people by putting my education in law to a different use, as a legislator. I made a commitment to run for office, and announced my candidacy for the first Nunavut elections in December 1998. My bar exams were finishing up, I knew that I was doing well and I had good support from the community.

From then on, I focused on getting elected, organizing my political campaign. I had a lot of respect for the two other candidates, Mr. Ben Ell and Mr. Matthew Spence. I felt that I had to earn my way. I worked really hard. I was lucky to have some good endorsements, like for example the mayor of the day, the late Flash Kilabuk, gave me an endorsement, for which I was very grateful.[6] He realized that we needed educated people to govern and that I had the credentials. He said, "You're Inuk, but you realize what challenges lie ahead for us. We need somebody like you to represent us." He was very up-front, he knew what he was doing.

Ben Ell was very clear, saying, "We weren't running against each other." We were running for office. I really appreciated his attitude, and I am proud of him. For my campaign, I went door-to-door a number of times, talked to people throughout the riding. I focused on my platform. Education was always my priority. It was one area that the territorial government had control over, that we can do something about.

It was an active campaign, very respectful. There were three seats for Iqaluit; Ed Picco, Hunter Tootoo, and I were elected. They were my new colleagues on election night. Following the election I met with my new colleagues, and we discussed how the government was going to be formed. I was convinced by Mr. Tootoo to pursue the Premier's seat, at that time. I told him that in the history of the Northwest Territories government, premiers only served one term. But I was there for the long haul. The work we had to do would take more than one term. They said, "We can always work on that part when we come to it." I wanted to do everything I could, for my territory.

I had fulfilled my own dream, by becoming a lawyer. Anything else after that was a bonus! Being a Member of the Legislative Assembly, becoming premier, anybody could do that. It wasn't that special for me. It was something that had to be done, for me to continue to contribute to my territory, to use my education to make things happen. It was an adjustment. I became a public figure in a new government; it was a prime time.

Everybody in Nunavut had their own expectations, what they wanted to see from the government of the day. That was the real challenge: because we were a public government and we had to represent everybody. We had a new cabinet, I had to work with them, to try and make things work for our territory. Education, delivering services, recruiting staff, those were my challenges.

I visited many communities, and realized, "Oh, my goodness!" When I went to Pond Inlet at the school, I saw

Paul Okalik as the first Nunavut Premier on the day of the
first Nunavut Legislative Assembly session on April 1st, 1999.
(Photo: Pierre Dunnigan)

chairs and desks in the hallway. I asked, "Are they renovat-
ing or something?" They said, "No, that's the classroom!"
Then I went to the closet, and there were little kids studying in the closet. I said, "What are we doing? We are going
to fix this. I don't want to see this anymore." The following year, we rebuilt a number of schools, and also built
new ones. How are we going to advance, if our kids are
learning in the hallways? We made education a priority.
I remember, my Minister of Education had to step aside,
for personal reasons.[7] That happened in 2003. I took on
the Education Department for the time being. I boosted
the budget so we could take care of the schools. I said to
my colleagues, "If any of you disagree with this, you are
going to be the new Education Minister."

Coming from Ontario, where you get real first-class
everything, conditions in the Eastern Arctic were a shock
for me. It's a different country from the rest of Canada,
in terms of what you can expect, in services from your

government. There was no staff, no infrastructure. Where should we start? For me, everything starts with the classroom. When you have more educated people, you have more staff from the community. I wanted to invest in the people, and build it up from there. In time, you add to it, along the way.

It's easy to look back and be critical of what happened in the first years of the Government of Nunavut, but at the time I was just trying to make my government work. I inherited the system; I had to work with it. The division of assets and liabilities with the Northwest Territories government had already been negotiated by the Office of the Interim Commissioner.[8] I had no control over that. You had to work with what we were given, including the budget from the federal government. Of course, it came up short, with all the needs that we had. It would have been great to have more things in place, but for me, I couldn't do anything about that. I chose to focus on governing and do as much as I could with what we had.

During the first term, Ed Picco was my Minister of Health. I was impressed by Peter Kilabuk, my Minister of Sustainable Development. He had done very well. When I needed a new Minister of Education, I gave that responsibility to Minister Kilabuk. I wanted a strong Department of Education. He was the one who conducted the consultations to propose a new Education Act in that first term. It didn't work out, and that was unfortunate.[9] I was lucky to have members from the past government. Kelvin Ng was my finance minister. We worked well together. I appointed him Deputy Premier. We got things done together. Manitok Thompson was also formerly part of the Northwest Territories government as well. We had differing opinions here and there, but we found ways to work together. It was a government with fresh faces, but with some experience. I first appointed her Minister of Public Works, because I needed someone with experience. We didn't have much office space, for example, and we were decentralizing our government.[10] She wasn't necessarily happy about it, but I needed strength and stability, I needed to make sure things could get done properly. It took a while, but she fulfilled that mandate and then she was ready for something else.

We had to proceed with decentralization. Although the departments to be decentralized had been identified, the work hadn't been done. We had to adjust it, and make it work. For example, the Nunavut Implementation Commission had identified all the local wildlife officers to be stationed in Pond Inlet. But we needed those wildlife officers in the communities, to manage local wildlife issues.[11] We had to make the adjustment. I had to say to my colleagues, "As a cabinet, we have to be seen to be representing everyone, not favouring any one community. And Pond Inlet does not have enough government positions. So one of the communities will have to make a sacrifice, to adjust those numbers."

So we moved some positions from my hometown of Pangnirtung that had been designated there to Pond Inlet, and looked for something else for Pangnirtung to compensate for those job promises that had been made under the Nunavut Implementation Commission. It had to be done, to make the government work if we were to remain credible. That was a difficult time with my cabinet colleagues. Luckily, Minister Kilabuk was willing to face the challenge and help us.

It was a challenge, but we had to make the government work. We discussed it, among all members in Baker Lake, in June of 1999.[12] I presented my colleagues with options, saying, "We are working under the current system that we inherited, so how do you want to make adjustments? This is our time. We can make the government work any way we wish, at this point, because we're new and we're in a good spot." We committed to the system that we have today. Yes, traditionally we were sovereign as communities, living more in camps. We've been invaded by another system, another organization. We can't be sovereign locally anymore; we're working under a federal political system. There are two levels of government that deliver the services that we need today. We don't have the resources to spread it out to all the communities. We can't work with the Northwest Territories system of regional boards anymore. We now have one territory, with primarily an Inuit population; we need to focus our resources on improving our services to the people.

I grew up in Pangnirtung. I lived in Iqaluit for some time. I don't identify with the artificial boundaries that were put in place between the Kitikmeot, Kivalliq, and Baffin. I am very proud to say that I am from Nunavut.

One of our first decisions was regarding the time zone. It was done with good intentions, to unify the territory. Up to that point, we had a resolution from Nunavut Tunngavik asking us to unify in one time zone. I had been asked to work on it by a colleague from the western part of Nunavut. This was around fall of 1999. I wound up stuck with the matter. I tried to follow through on it. We tried it for a few months. There were some issues, so I said, "Forget it, and let's move on. We have other priorities."[13]

Our cabinet decisions had to be consensual. In 2003, we were considering moving some divisions from Rankin Inlet, which was doing very well under decentralization.

One of my cabinet colleagues went public with the matter, and that beached our efforts, and I had to make a decision. I stripped that colleague of his portfolios, to maintain my authority and keep my cabinet intact.[14] It was a difficult time. My colleagues in the legislative assembly supported my decision. I was working to keep the cabinet strong and unified; to follow through with the decisions we arrived at, with authority, with solidarity. Everyone made sacrifices to make decentralization work.

Kekerten Harbour, site of a former whaling station, and bowhead whale jaw as a memorial to the hunt by Inuit in 1998, July 2007.
(Photo: Bernd Gieseking)

CHAPTER 5

My Role Was to Lead
and Make Things Work

We were a new government, coming in after the planning work of the Nunavut Implementation Commission and inheriting decisions already made by the Office of the Interim Commissioner. After the creation of Nunavut in 1999, we launched a round of consultations in all the communities. All these consultations resulted in the Bathurst Mandate.[1]

That declaration was the result of what Nunavut people saw as their priorities for the new territorial government in the long run. It required a lot of deliberations for the cabinet. We made education and housing our two major priorities. Some members wanted more. I said, "I want our government to focus, I want to deliver on two areas. Not five or six. The bureaucrats won't know what we want to focus on, if we have too many priorities." We all agreed that those two areas needed to be addressed quickly.

The issue of the language of the government that should be Inuktitut by 2020 was included in the Bathurst mandate; that same year, Nunavut government workforce should be 85 percent Inuit. We set those goals. Our plan was that with education as a priority we'll get Inuit working in the government, and get them qualified. Everything flows from there. I made it clear that I was there for my government, and not for personal gain. I put strict rules and conditions on my colleagues who had business interests to not touch any matter related to their private business. And it worked, we made it work. Under my government, there were no scandals.

Unfortunately, before the creation of Nunavut, the Northwest Territories government sold off some public housing assets. We had no control over that. They needed the money to finance their issues of the day. The Office of the Interim Commissioner saw that, and signed leases for the level of employees we had, up to that point, for staff housing. When Nunavut came to be, we had no more public housing and no more assets in the Department of Public Works. But we had to find housing and office space for our new employees, and rapidly. We also had a big increase in the number of our civil servants. We had to recruit new staff.

For example, the Sivummut building, the education building, was originally scheduled to be leased. But I said, "Who's going to occupy it?" If my government was going to be the only one occupying it, then it made more sense to buy it, instead of leasing, and paying a third party for office space.

I was always very supportive of consensus decision-making for government. My role was to lead and make things work. I did not always agree with what was decided, but my job was to make sure that the cabinet decisions were followed through. For example, the generosity of compensation and pensions for the ministers was something I couldn't support; but it was a cabinet decision, so I had to go along with it. It was decided by the majority. I had to live with the outcome.

It was not all that difficult for me to adjust to a big apparatus such as the government structure. I had had more challenges than that in my life; this was just another one. It was something that had to be done. At that point in my life, I was close to a number of elders, and they were very helpful, in making sure that I was staying grounded. The late Simon Tookoomee, from Baker Lake, was one of my justices of the peace. I had known him since before Nunavut was created.[2] I often sought his advice in difficult circumstances. He was always very gracious and understanding. Also Jimmy Makpah, an Anglican minister from Pond Inlet. Whenever he knew I was in a difficult situation, he would get in touch with me and help me stay strong for our territory. There were very good people caring for me during those times. I felt very vulnerable at times.

Nunavut Tunngavik Inc. acted as a watchdog over the land claims implementation process. We had a good relationship, overall. I was always fighting for Inuit even though I was the premier of a public government. Our Inuit population continues to be at the bottom of the social ladder. Even though we're a public government, we have a duty to look after those who are the most vulnerable in our territory. I always went above and beyond the Nunavut Land Claims Agreement, to elevate the standard of living for those who were the most vulnerable. When it came to apply Nunavummi Nangminiqaqtunik Ikajuuti (NNI policy), contracting territorial parks for example, we always pushed my government to go further than those commitments to the Land Claims Agreement, to have a positive contribution to the Inuit of the territory.[3] I never found it a burden or a challenge, to work with Nunavut Tunngavik Inc. Even if the leaders changed here and there, the obligations of the Government of Nunavut continued.

My most frustrating issue with NTI was trying to have them relocate their business corporations to Nunavut. Every business entity that you see elsewhere has its head office in the jurisdiction where they work, and that is where they pay taxes. Nunasi Corp. was headquartered in Yellowknife, and it pretended to work for the development of Nunavut Inuit? I had a real quarrel with them, asking them to relocate anywhere in Nunavut, and make a substantial contribution by paying taxes to Nunavut. The other Corporation is the Nunavut Trust, which managed compensation money for the territory. It's in Ottawa, of all places! I said, "Look! It's a billion dollars that's being taxed in Ontario! We're not benefiting from that!" They're still in Ontario. I just shake my head. That's not what we wanted. The territory should at least benefit from the tax dollars they generate.

I didn't always agree with Arctic co-operatives either, because their federation is headquartered in Winnipeg.

The German Chancellor Helmut Kohl came for a visit just before the creation of the territory. Jacques Chirac was our first foreign visitor, in September of 1999. This helped us to develop our ties to tourism. We were always trying to look for ways to improve. He had a personal interest in Inuit art. It was also important because French is an official language in our territory. Chirac helped us to see what we could work on, together. I met with his minister for tourism, a number of times. And France has the only Inuktitut school, outside of the territory. They are doing better than us![4]

Human rights legislation was a big issue on the tail end of my first term. I am very proud of that legislation, even though it went against the grain of public sentiment. I feel very strongly that we need to protect the rights of all minorities.[5]

Paul Okalik with the late Simon Tookoomee, who advised Paul
in the early stages.

CHAPTER 6

You Have to Be Decisive, and Act Quickly

Everyday, in the interest of our government, our people, and our territory we have to make decisions so that our government will be the strongest and the most credible it can be. Finding the right balance is the challenge.

In March of 1999, the new Government of Nunavut was sworn in. Right away, I was busy making sure the right people got hired for each department. I was trying to figure out how to make our administration work with all these service contracts previously signed by the Office of the Interim Commissioner: contracts with the senior civil servants, the deputy ministers, leases, and things like that. As of April 1999, we only had fifty government employees! Maintaining services was our number one priority. At the very beginning we had a series of agreements with the Northwest Territories government to deliver most of our services. Our newly created government just didn't have the capacity to provide them yet.

I wondered how all this was going to work? How would we get full control over our decisions? How long were these contracts signed for? When would we be able to hire our own people, and deliver services ourselves? I insisted that we hire as many Inuit as we could, and that we provide them a good training. We started at a low 40 percent of Inuit employment, and as we managed to double the number of government employees, we increased the number of Inuit workers as well, up to 50 percent plus. For my second term, we reached around 54 percent of Inuit employment in the Government of Nunavut, at all levels. The approach we used is called 'direct appointments.'[1] We used that approach only for Inuit. After I left, the government changed that, and opened it up to anybody, again. The number of Inuit working in government went back down, which was a real disappointment to me. For example, during my terms, we wouldn't even consider a cabinet direct appointment for a non-Inuit. We were working to get our levels up of Inuit employees. I had one-on-one discussions with my ministers, making it clear what I expected from the departments. I had to use my authority to decide, to emphasize what we held as a priority.

As a public government, you have to be fair with everyone. At the same time, the Canadian Charter of Rights and Freedoms that we work under has special provisions for indigenous peoples, who have been discriminated against in the past. We have the responsibility to try bringing them to the same level of quality of life as any other Canadian. We used the Canadian Charter of Rights and Freedoms to access programs and support for Nunavut Inuit.

We have invested in special post-secondary programs such as the Akitsiraq Law School, the nursing and education programs. We also increased tuition assistance for students. We built new schools and made improvements to existing ones. We probably will need to do more to increase opportunities for Inuit in the Nunavut government. What we've done is still not enough. We need to instil confidence in the younger generation of Inuit, that they can do whatever they set their mind to and that our public system will support them. They have to get the confidence to push themselves.

I had to use my authority to make decisions that I believed were in the best interest of our territory. I made sure we had a strong government that could deliver on its commitments. I used my authority to remove people who were not productive, to make tough decisions to shuffle ministers, and always make changes in the best interests of the territory. I had my critics, and still do today. But I grew up in a tougher neighbourhood than that. Nunavut is my community and I will always carry out my mandate to the best I can.

I pushed for tax breaks for hunting and mining training programs. We supported the opening of a mine in Baker Lake, which created a lot of opportunities for people in that area.[2] It wasn't necessarily popular with some ministers, but I felt that we needed to create opportunities. Kivalliq Inuit are still benefiting from the mine, and that's great for the territory. It meant jobs, opportunities to train new workers, and when that mine will shut down, workers can go back to their communities and operate heavy equipment, or work as mechanics. These were new opportunities for Inuit, in a different area.

Decentralization was also an important strategy of both my terms in power. To some extent, it was unpopular—although it was well received by the communities. It was the people who had to be displaced, who were unhappy, basically. We had plans to put in place, and we had to make important adjustments.

I gathered my cabinet, and asked each member, "What can we do for this community, and this other one? We're going to be short of this many positions for this community, for example..." I would send them back to their departments, and asked them to come back later in the afternoon with a list of positions they could decentralize. Communities such as Pangnirtung, or Pond Inlet, or Igloolik had never seen such government services operating in their communities. They only had maybe three government jobs in their communities. We brought in more than fifty to sixty people in each decentralized community. It was difficult, and costly, to make that happen. We had made a commitment to decentralize the government administration and I'm very proud that we did it. The level of unemployment in those communities is much higher than in Iqaluit and the influx of government jobs was very much welcomed. The communities are really happy. But we had to manage communication. We had to consider the employees that were impacted and consult with them to make sure that they were aware of the move, without revealing the broader plan. We were offering those employees the proper assistance if they chose to relocate, alternate employment if they chose to stay, or the option to retire or resign. That transition was a very sensitive issue. It was a good challenge to make sure the communities benefited from our government. We worked hard to honour the plan that was put in place by the Nunavut Implementation Commission.

The government presence in these communities has a positive impact on the residents; when I was growing up in Pangnirtung all you saw was the welfare office, the wildlife officers, and that was it.

I don't recall much of the discussion about rewriting the existing Northwest Territories Education Act during

The Nunavut Legislative Assembly (Photo: Louis McComber)

my first term as Premier. We tried to improve it, but this new version of the Act wasn't acceptable to the regular Members of the Legislative Assembly. We learned from that experience. I appointed a strong Minister of Education for our second term, the Hon. Ed Picco, to make sure we did it right. I told Minister Picco, "During this term, I want an Education Act." Could he get it done in two years? "No. You need more time, to consult. Let's work at it as long as we need to." First, we worked on a consultation plan. We took the time to listen to the people, and the end result was a plan which we felt was the very best for our territory.

The second Education Act proposed a bilingual system, with Inuktitut being taught from kindergarten through grade twelve. Inuit wanted more Inuktitut in the education system. Our government had to be able to function in both languages. I would actually prefer even a trilingual system. The more languages you know, the easier it is to find work, regardless of which government it might be. *J'espère qu'on peut avoir les trois langues dans le terri-toire.* This is something now that I'd love to see happening. But we simply cannot get enough Inuit teachers to teach Inuktitut to an acceptable academic standard in schools, at a level that would allow graduates entrance into university or college. We have to maintain the credentials for our education system that will bring our kids to post-secondary education.

Under the current system, some kids are still doing well. They're moving on to medical school, law school, or an academic curriculum of their choice. The education system is allowing our students to succeed. But the Inuktitut component still needs to be improved, for students to have a strong foundation in both languages. As an Inuk, that's what gave me the strength to succeed: the foundation that I was given by my family. I used it and it helped me to survive. I'd like to see more Inuit succeed, in whatever field they may choose. Parents are crucial, to give young people the push they need, to succeed. If it wasn't for my own mother, I would never have continued on. Today, I push my own children, to try and get as much education as they can. That's my job, as a parent: to make sure they get the best they can, and do better.

I'm encouraged by what I see. When I visit high schools, I am encouraged by the level of questions students are asking and their interest in going to university. I think we'll do better in the coming years. It's looking good.

Sometimes, I had to make decisions that didn't necessarily have the support of my cabinet colleagues. But I had to maintain control, remain confident, and deliver on those decisions. It was always respectful, confidential. I still had to make decisions. Over the first term, I lost a few ministers: one found it too challenging, another one had problems with the law and he took the honourable step and chose to resign from cabinet, which made my decision easier.

The next one was Minister Jack Anawak, when he spoke publicly about our cabinet discussions.[3] He broke the cabinet confidentiality. I went to see him and said, "At this time tomorrow, I'm going to announce that you have no more portfolios. You have the option to resign, but it's up to you." He chose not to resign. The caucus decided to put forward a motion to remove him from cabinet. That demonstrated solidarity.

The following term had a number of resignations, too. Another difficult situation was when I found that my Minister of Finance had been carrying out private business, using his ministerial office.[4] It had been made clear that elected members shouldn't do that. I was made aware of an email message sent from his office, in which he was trying to promote his private interests on government time. At the time, he was en route to a finance ministers' conference in Winnipeg. I called him right away, and told him I would be making an official announcement the next day. I gave him the option, to step aside and return home immediately. He couldn't represent my territory as our Minister of Finance anymore. To maintain the government credibility, and demonstrate that we put the interests of the territory before individual interests, I had to act. I gave him twenty-four hours to step aside, or I was going to go public. He did the honourable thing and stepped aside. In terms of the public pressures of the job, I had good support from my caucus. In difficult situations, this made my actions easier. I felt less alone because the burden wasn't just on me. It had to be done for our territory. You have to be decisive, and act quickly.

CHAPTER 7

It's Still Taking Us Too Long to Catch Up

I appointed Minister Ed Picco as the Education Minister for my second term. Mr. Picco had worked hard in the Department of Health, for the previous term, and I wanted to keep one Minister of Education throughout all of the second term. I wanted to instil stability for that department. I told Ed, "We need an education bill that can work for our territory." He wanted to do it within two years, and I said, "We have to consult broadly and make sure it's done properly, so take the time. Two years is too short. We need to dedicate resources and the time to make sure we do it properly." By the end of the term, we had a rather broadly-supported education bill that was workable for our territory.

We wanted to have a strong bilingual education, trilingual when possible, but to this day, we don't have the qualified teachers. The Inuktitut-speaking teachers to implement the legislation are not there yet. So that's the unfortunate part. If we can get more Inuktitut-speaking teachers who can speak and teach in Inuktitut, then we'll create a very strong foundation for our traditional language. That part still needs to be addressed. We made the commitment of up to grade eight, grade nine for sure, and then high school level, whenever we have the teaching complement. We're still not there, unfortunately.

We consulted as broadly as possible, with many people, and I recall the Standing Committee also travelled throughout the territory to hear from people on the proposed bill.[1] During the final legislative stage, we had almost weekly committee meetings to fine-tune the bill, with the work of the Standing Committee and our government.

We worked with the Francophone community as well, on the French language component. I'm impressed by the work that the Francophone community does to ensure that French is going to survive and thrive in our territory. I learned from the good work of the Francophone community as to what we need to do for Inuktitut, for example. I appreciate the contributions that the Francophones are making for our territory. They're hard working, and they understand the challenges we face for our own language. For example, having one telephone number for government French services is a great idea. I told my departments, "Let's have one phone number for Inuktitut services too, because we have unilingual Inuit who should be getting government services in their language." Particularly in Nunavut, the Inuit homeland.

We inherited eleven official languages from the former territorial administration, so it was a bit of a challenge for us to address that. I'm very pleased that we were able to work with the federal government on this language issue; because of the Canadian Official Languages Act of 1969, the federal consent was required to change our territorial language legislation. We worked with all the communities in Nunavut as well, making sure that we had the best language legislation for our territory. Even though we're a territorial jurisdiction, the Constitution of Canada requires the federal government to ensure that English and French remain the official languages in the territory. We have to work with what we have. I was pleased that they understood that Inuktitut should have the same status as the other Canadian official languages in Nunavut. A motion had to be passed through Parliament, as well as consented by the Senate.[2]

Inuktut is being widely used in many western Nunavut communities such as Taloyoak and Kugaaruk in the Kitikmeot.[3] I travelled there and they are still very fluent in Inuinaqtun.[4] In Kugluktuk, it is spoken mostly by elders. In Cambridge Bay, I know that the language is a challenge. They still use their language in Gjoa Haven. In the Kivalliq region, Baker Lake is one community that is a concern, but in the rest of the region the Inuit language remains strong. In Coral Harbour, all the young people speak Inuktitut. I went to their high school, and they very well understood me in Inuktitut. On Baffin Island, the capital city Iqaluit needs a bit more help, and Resolute Bay, unfortunately, is a real challenge. In the rest of Baffin, Inuktitut is quite strong. We have to continue to use it and strengthen it, to make sure our language survives. We have to come up with more solutions to strengthen it.

We have two writing systems, and it's just not viable. In a modern society, we have to use technology to communicate, and we have to adapt our language accordingly. We have to utilize the Roman alphabet to text and use our language in the modern means of communication. That's one area we're working on, as a government. We'll keep using the syllabic orthography for the elders, but if we want the younger generation to use our language, we have to adapt our writing system to their way of life.

For official legal documents, we have authoritative languages in Nunavut for the time being, English and French, because we don't have Inuktitut-speaking lawyers who can draft Inuktitut legislation yet. That will be a proud day for me, when we will have an Inuktitut version of our legislation that we can go to court with, and that will be interpreted by the courts. That's one day I look forward to see, as a lawyer and as an Inuk. We have a long way to go to really be a truly trilingual territory!

Visiting Greenland, I was encouraged to see that their focus on language and culture was supported by a special school, the Knud Rasmussen Folk High School, to make sure that their culture flourishes in our globalized world.[5] Minister Louis Tapardjuk was quite keen on seeing that our language and our culture were strengthened in Greenland, and I was very supportive of his efforts to create something similar in Nunavut.[6] He wanted to make sure that we had a school, to teach about our culture and strengthen our language. He was very helpful in pushing in that direction. He should take the compliment for the establishment of the Nunavut cultural school, Piqqusilirivvik Inuit Cultural Learning Centre, but also the adoption of the language bills.[7] We asked for feasibility studies to determine the best location for such a school. I made a commitment that we would locate new facilities into smaller communities. Clyde River was an ideal place to have the cultural school, and I'm very pleased to see that it was built there. I'd like to see more push in that direction, to learn more about our past and how we can use that ancestral heritage today. Like in areas of conflict resolution, I think it could be a real help for our government and our territory. I would like to go there and visit myself, and see how it's going. We also committed to satellite campuses in the communities of Igloolik and Baker Lake. From what I know, it can be very helpful especially to people ending up in difficult situations, carrying anger and despair from past experiences. In our culture, you shouldn't carry those burdens—"Let them go. You can have a more productive life!" I was very blessed to go through that experience, and let go of that anger, and I moved on to a healthier lifestyle, for example. Tapping in our heritage could be very useful today; we should use our culture more to have a healthier society.

During my challenging days, I was very fortunate to be able to count on calling elders like the late Simon Tookoomee; he was very wise. I would call and ask him, "What am I going through here?" He wouldn't direct me, but he would provide good advice, referring to how certain events have occurred in the past. He was very good in that way. I would also count on the late Jimmy Makpah, who was originally from Pond Inlet, but who spent time in Pangnirtung where I grew up. He resided in Arviat, and he was a very strong individual. He was very helpful for me, during my difficult days of governing. So I must say that I was very fortunate to be able to count on elders. Near the end of my term as Premier as well, I had relatives here in Iqaluit who were elderly, and when I was trying to figure out what to do after my term, I went to my cousin's other half here in Iqaluit. I asked him, "What do I do now?" He pointed out to me, "You're an Inuk, but you also have an education that makes you aware of things that we don't see. You use both, and make us think of things we never thought of. That is a gift that you should use to help our fellow citizens." That really renewed my commitment to serve my fellow Inuit here in our territory. They have been very good to me, and I appreciate their work.

I would feel lost without the elderly assisting me in my political roles. Sometimes, some very good people called me and said, "What are you doing?" And I would explain, "I'm part of a minority, and I understand that minority discrimination takes place, and I don't enjoy that.[8] We Inuit are a minority. We may be a majority in our territory, but we're a minority group in Canada, and we do not like being discriminated against. So that's where I'm coming from: I do not want any minority group being discriminated against." And they would understand why I was in that predicament. So, yes, of course they call, and I explain my situation. We don't always agree, but at least we talk and discuss why we are taking these stands.

When I encounter people on my way, their comments are not always negative! They are mostly very positive comments. I like walking as a way of relieving stress, and then you encounter people, and they encourage you to keep working and making decisions that may not always be popular. A lot of times, they will call now and again, if they have a different point of view. Most times, it's encouraging words, to keep up the good work. I appreciate that.

Considering that Inuit are the majority in Nunavut, we have to do something as a government to make sure that Inuit catch up to the rest of the country. I have no issue with prioritizing Inuit employment and training in our territory, and that will continue to be my position. Until the day we are all on the same level as the rest of our citizens here in our territory, I do not even consider critics of discrimination. I see my fellow Inuit suffering, and they need help. I will continue to do my utmost to make sure that they get the same level of education where possible, training, and employment opportunities where we can. Unfortunately, we're not there yet. We have about 85 percent of Inuit in our territory, and we're still at 50 percent today in our government Inuit employment. So we're not even close, and we've been struggling with that for a while. I do not really care about what people say about our government in that area, because we have to do our part. A working Inuk is a far more positive contribution to the overall territory than an unemployed, uneducated Inuk. That's how I view it. People should see that, regardless of their background. As a government, we don't want any part of our territory and our citizens suffering. Yes, it's great to learn more about our language. At the same time, we're trying to make sure that our citizens have the same level of education as anywhere else, so that they can qualify for university or college. That will continue to be a challenge for coming generation of Inuit.

When we'll get educated enough to assume all these responsibilities as Inuit, that will be the day when we can fully meet our expectations. Unfortunately, that takes a bit of time. I go to all the high schools wherever I can and explain to those young students, "I need you working, and you have to get educated for us to get you working in our government." I explain to them, I happen to be an Inuk, just like you. And I'm a lawyer. It's just a matter of committing to it and working hard to get there. I tell that to every student, wherever I can. We have had some success, but not enough. I never thought I'd see an Inuk doctor; now we have one. We have an Inuk veterinarian here in our community—same level as a doctor. So those things are slowly coming along. We're showing the world that Inuit are capable of achieving these things, as long as they're committed to their education. I'm encouraged, but it's still taking us too long to catch up.

CHAPTER 8

I Don't Just Sit There and Smile and Clap My Hands

The 2008 election was a challenging time, because even if we had done as much work as we could in the previous administration, some people didn't appreciate what we were trying to do. There were some important political changes after the election of the Eva Aariak government, and I was at the receiving end of a lot of people's frustration. So I didn't carry the day. That was unfortunate. My government had raised the level of Inuit employment to about 54 percent of our overall Government of Nunavut total employment. During the next five years, our level of Inuit employment went down. That's the price to pay for electing people who may not have been ready to govern.[1]

I was used to governing, and I was very much aware of the challenges that the new administration was facing. I took part in the discussion as a regular member when the government was setting priorities. They wanted to set ten priorities, and I said, "How is that going to work? How are you going to focus on getting things done, when you have so many priorities?" When you have too many priorities, you don't really have priorities. It can be a challenge to accomplish anything. *C'est la vie!* What did this last government accomplish? I don't know, really. It had no focus. That was my main comment early on. Leading up to the review of the government, I was applying my knowledge of governing, criticizing where I saw a real lack of leadership on current issues.[2] Making announcements on accomplishments that they didn't have any role initiating was something that I couldn't agree with. At least they should have mentioned the previous minister who was there, who started the project and made sure it happened. Don't just take credit for things that you didn't have anything to do with! That's something I found a bit of an issue for me and for past colleagues who worked very hard to make those things happen.

There were a lot of events and controversies leading up to these political changes; it's the price to pay for making decisions. I made decisions that added up to some people not being very happy. So what? That's what you do as the head of a government; you have to make decisions, and move on. Some people may not always agree with your decisions, but for me, it's about moving on and making sure that we're in the direction that we want to go. My role was to govern and make decisions, and I didn't rule just by myself. I worked with my cabinet colleagues, and made use of their knowledge and their resources, to make things happen, and to make things move. That's what I'm known for. I don't just sit there and smile and clap my hands. I actually do work, show up for work, and consider each recommendation coming from the various levels of government, and review them, and assess them, and come up with my own decision. I don't just rely on advice. I review all of the impacts that my decision might have on my territory. I don't just accept recommendations;

I actually consider them, and look at the best interests of my territory. That's my job as a Minister, and that was my job as the leader of our government. A lot of the time, I would not agree with what was coming before cabinet. I would talk to my cabinet colleagues and explain, "This is my concern on this issue." I would not put it before cabinet until we work things out to make it work better. Some people may view that as an unfortunate way of governing, but my job was to make sure that we come up with the best decisions possible for our territory, and I continue to have that view. I do whatever I can to help my fellow citizens, in whatever role I have.

After the 2008 election, I became a regular member of the Legislative Assembly. I wanted to take some time, and review what my future options might be. I looked at the numbers and realized that even if I stood up to try to get to Cabinet, I would not have the numbers to be elected in. I thought, "They want a change, let them have a change!" I accepted my role as a regular member. I'm very pleased that I did that, because looking at the record of the Aariak government: did they accomplish anything? It's hard to pinpoint much accomplishment in the five years that they spent in government. I do not want to be associated with that type of work, because I believe in having a role and being an active person in government. As a regular member, I was the first member of the Legislative Assembly ever to pass a private member's bill, which is the Order of Nunavut that we are using very proudly today.[3] I worked with our Commissioner of the day, the Honourable Ann Meekitjuk Hanson, to put that legislation in place, and I'm very proud of that work.

I was assessing what to do. I wanted to continue to serve Nunavut in whatever capacity. When the speaker's position came up, I said I'll give it a try, but it was not for me. James Arreak was our speaker in our second term in power, and he was then appointed to a cabinet position. I viewed it as an opportunity to do what I could for my territory. I'm used to working and making sure that I hold the government to account, or serving in the government and doing my part. I found it frustrating to stay in my new speaker position.

I was assessing my future, and a federal election was looming. I looked at the platforms of the different parties, and the Liberal Party was stressing that they wanted to help aboriginal Canadians in education; something that I really agreed with. The new leader Michael Ignatieff was stressing education, and more specifically aboriginal education, something that I fully support and agree with. Paul Martin had supported the Kelowna Accord, and the Harper Conservative government just threw it away.[4] I did not agree with that at all, so when the Liberal Party under Ignatieff stressed aboriginal education, I said okay. I want to do my part and make sure we support our fellow aboriginal Canadians, particularly Inuit, in getting more education support. I met with Michael Ignatieff that summer, when he was looking for a candidate, and I was considering my options. He came to Iqaluit. I threw my hat in for candidacy for the Liberal Party in the 2011 election. But Nunavummiut mostly felt that they wanted to be part of the ruling government, and they voted for the Conservative candidate, Leona Aglukkaq.

I didn't agree with the entire Liberal platform; gun control was something that really was not agreeable for any of us. That was an important hindrance for my candidacy. Ignatieff continued to stress gun control, and that did not go down well with the Nunatsiaq constituents. We saw the same impact in the Yukon riding, as well.[5] I'm very pleased with Mr. Justin Trudeau just saying, "No, this is not an issue, let's move on!" I'm sure the North has heard that.

I was accountable to all, in my previous capacity as the Premier of the territory. I didn't see running for a territory-wide body as any different, because I had run in electoral campaigns for quite some time. I was just stressing the federal programs and options that our constituents could consider, and why I was running; for me it was for aboriginal education.

I view Nunavut as one territory.[6] There are three artificial boundaries that were introduced for administrative purposes early on by the Northwest Territories government, Baffin, Kivalliq, and Kitikmeot, but this is really only one territory. Nunavummiut chose to be a part of the ruling government, and to benefit from that government, and that was pretty much the outcome of the 2011 election. That's how it turned out! What can you do?

Criminal law is a federal responsibility, and it really is a burden for Inuit, as it prevents us from doing positive things for our fellow citizens. There are a number of areas that are under federal jurisdiction, that really impact our territory. Our ability to generate revenue is also federally determined. As Inuit and aboriginals, as a part of Canada, we're supposed to get federal assistance. That's pretty much nothing, not much at all. Even though gun control was the big issue of the day, our land claims agreement is still there today. The gun registry may have disappeared, but the Nunavut Land Claims Agreement is still being breached by the federal government, towards Inuit.[7] Those things are occurring. It was a big, big issue, made out to be a very big issue during the election, that the Conservative government would abolish the gun registry. Sure, the registry may be gone, but Inuit are still required to have a licence to have a gun. Under the Nunavut Land Claims Agreement, Inuit are supposed to be able to hunt freely, without a licence or fees. The federal legislation still requires that an Inuk who wants to hunt and who wants to buy ammunition should have a gun licence. That's against the Nunavut Land Claims Agreement. That's counter to the promises that were made by the Conservative party in the 2011 election. It's still in effect! For me today, to go hunting in my territory, I need to have a licence to get ammunition for my rifle. To get that licence, you need not to have a criminal record. And you have to pay fees, in order to apply for that licence. My aboriginal rights have been breached today, by the federal government. Those are things that should be addressed.

I did not agree with the decision of the last government of removing Minister Louis Tapardjuk from Cabinet, because he could have been very useful in making sure our traditional point of view was considered in the Department of Justice.[8] I questioned that decision, because you need to assess all options, and look at the problem as a whole, not just a narrow perspective. For us to solve it, as a government, we had to consider all options and listen to all views, regardless of whether you agree with it or not, for us to consider, to make changes.

I'm now blessed with colleagues who are committed to working for my territory and making a difference, so I'm very fortunate to have colleagues who are committed to the same goals as me. Education is a continuing priority for me, and for Nunavut, it's a priority of our government, for example. It's something that we hope that we can tackle together.

CHAPTER 9

Southern Canada Did Not Get Developed Without National Support

I worked hard building productive relationships with my colleagues from other territories and provinces, primarily from western Canada. I and Premier Gary Doer of Manitoba were elected premiers on the same year, and we worked so well together.[1] We supported each other on many occasions; I was very impressed with him. Even though issues didn't involve his province, he would get on my side and support my efforts by influencing other premiers. At our annual First Ministers' conference, aboriginal issues were my main focus, and Premier Doer would be right there with me, making sure we addressed and pushed the national agenda on that front. When we were struggling at the national table, we from the territories aimed at health care. He was there for us, asking the federal government to give us more per capita than the rest of the country because we didn't have the basic resources, and he understood our challenges.

I remember when Prime Minister Jean Chrétien was holding the First Ministers' conference on health care. I was the senior premier of the three northern territories for the conference.[2] Prime Minister Chrétien was very firm and difficult for all of us. We had new premiers elected in Ontario and Quebec at the time. The Ontario Conservative Premier Ernie Eves was representing the province with the largest population to be impacted.[3] Chrétien said, "I have two documents: one saying yes to what I'm proposing, and one saying no. If you say no, you get nothing!" So that left us in a bit of a predicament. None of us were getting what we wanted for our level of health care spending. We had a quick caucus, and Chrétien said, "I'm giving you two minutes to decide." So we had two minutes to discuss. He had given us what he was offering in terms of money, and for Nunavut it was going to be two million dollars for the year, in additional health care money; something we would spend in a week! Two million dollars was going to have no impact for us, even with a small population base. So we asked Premier Eves to go talk to Jean Chrétien, on behalf of us, to get a discussion going. He came back within five minutes saying, "No, Chrétien is not moving." So we had nowhere else to go. I and my colleagues from the North couldn't agree to accept that offer. When Chrétien came back to the room, the rest of the premiers accepted the deal, but they told the Prime Minister that the North was not accepting this. We walked out; we left. We went to the media room and held our own press conference. We told the country that we were saying 'no' to the Prime Minister on this one. So we did not sign on. We had discussed this before, and we had agreed that we could live without it, without raising false expectations for our population. From there we began new discussions, but

Premier Gary Doer, of all the premiers, spoke for us at the national table and said, "They aren't asking for much, but what little we offer them as a country has a real impact for them, so we should listen to them and accept their modest proposal." I was very proud of him.

We resumed discussions, and that's how the Access Health Program was created, with twenty million dollars of additional funding, which we used for medical travel primarily. So that's how that fund was created. It's been over ten years now, so that's over 200 million for the territory in terms of health care. So it has helped, but it took a national conference to make that happen. We get a transfer payment like the rest of the country, pretty much a little more per capita for health care than the provinces. The new agreement was targeted for health services. We get it in instalments with a five-year commitment and annual instalments for the territory.

Another thing that occurred at the First Ministers' conferences was the support to build a road to Nunavut which was the first commitment from my colleagues when I first attended a provincial/territorial meeting.[4] That was really special!

The most impact of our premiers' network was when the United States closed their border on all cattle meat products coming from Canada, because of the threat of the mad cow disease in Alberta.[5] But they also banned imports of caribou and musk ox meat that Nunavut was exporting to the United States at the time. I discussed the case with my premier colleagues, and said, "We have nothing to do with that mad cow disease. We have none of that. These are all wild animals, and there's no reason for them catching any of this stuff. They're only being banned because they're Canadian meat products." My colleagues agreed with our position, and Manitoba again was very strong in our corner. We agreed that we would release this information across Canada. From there I went straight to the United States Ambassador's office, and said, "I need your help reopening the border for our caribou and musk ox meat exports to the United States." Within the week, the border was re-opened for our Nunavut meat products. I'm still very proud of that. Even though we may be small, we were able to have an impact on an international decision. There's a high turnover amongst the Canadian premiers, so I became more senior, and had more voice and experience than my colleagues, so I used it to support our efforts as a territory.

Jean Chrétien was tough, but he was able to move his government towards what we really needed. We thought we needed support. Paul Martin was a lot more amenable, and he just accepted to consider the needs of the North on health care when he became Prime Minister. He also began working with us on a national accord on aboriginal issues.[6] At first, I had no strong expectations of him, but these discussions really convinced me that he was committed to assist us in tackling our challenges. I was very proud of that. Unfortunately, that was just two months before his government was defeated.[7] In our first meeting with Prime Minister Harper, I stressed very strongly that we needed to implement the Kelowna Accord on aboriginal issues.[8] We needed to make sure it continues, regardless of which government was in place. Stephen Harper did not acknowledge what they were going to do at the time. After we met with him, we realized that he wasn't going to honour the Kelowna Accord. So that was very unfortunate. It would have been a very good accord, and it did not occur.

I had a good rapport with Quebec premiers, regardless of which party it was, because we wanted to work on

French issues, as a trilingual territory, so it was always a very positive working relationship with any party in power in Quebec. Our relationship improved especially with Jean Charest as Premier; we had very good discussions in terms of climate change and aboriginal issues. I've always been very pleased with our connections to Quebec. We have an ongoing agreement with them to assist us in French terminology for health services, for example. So it's been a good, positive relationship.

I would travel to Europe as part of the federal delegation attacking anti-sealing each year, and we would meet with European parliamentarians and explain the potential consequences of a ban on sealskin products for Nunavut. I would tell our story as aboriginal people, as Inuit who rely heavily on sealskin to continue our harvesting practices. We were successful in holding off a vote on a sealskin ban from Europe for a number of years. But after the 2008 change in our territorial council, those trips were discontinued.[9] The outcome was a European vote to ban sealskins from Canada.

So that was some of the work I did externally, to represent my territory. Some of the discussions were successful, and some of them we are still working on, such as an agreement on federal devolution and a road to Nunavut. Those discussions are still ongoing, and hopefully one day we'll see success on these issues.

We had really good relations with Greenland, in terms of trying to support each other's efforts. We're not that successful in our Inuit education system, and Greenland is, but Greenland has struggled with wildlife management, and we have done well at it, so we exchange information to help each other in strengthening our structures. They had a twenty-year head start on us, with their Home

Rule Government.[10] They've had very good experience in strengthening their language, getting Inuit in government and in the workforce. We are very pleased with their work. Their national government of Denmark has been far more supportive of their efforts. They have a devolution agreement, and they control their fisheries. We don't have any of that. They have received a lot of transfer payments to build up their infrastructure; they have nice seaports, for example. We have none of that. So those are things that we will continue to struggle for, until our own government realizes that we are a part of Canada. Southern Canada did not get developed without national support. We're waiting for that to arrive here in our territory.

It would be nice to see some federal government support, for at least a few basic infrastructure needs that we have, so that Nunavut can be a part of our country and contribute to developing our economy. We have no facilities to receive any boats, other than to anchor out there and take days to unload! They can't really load anything. Those are things that I see happening in Greenland which we don't see happening here.

When Harper announced a port near Iqaluit during one of his campaigns, we said, "Okay, good; we're finally getting a deep seaport!" And then he said, "Okay, we'll look at it later." Then he announced that the port would be at Nanisivik, how's that going to help us? It's not going to add to any of our infrastructure; it's already there! There was already a marine port there for an old mining site.[11] How is that going to add to what we need to assist us unloading ships here, for example? We were shutting down that road from Nanisivik to Arctic Bay. How's that going to help Arctic Bay? I have lost interest in these empty promises, I must say. They just haven't been met.

Nunavut needs some seaports, not just for Iqaluit but for other communities as well, because we won't build any roads, on the island, for example. Our only real means of transporting big equipment is by boat, so we need some financial support there. And for us to develop our fisheries further, it would be nice to have more facilities such as ports and docks, in places like Qikiqtarjuaq or Clyde River, that have potential for fisheries. They catch about fifty million dollars' worth of shrimp outside Qikiqtarjuaq and Clyde River. But that renewable resource cannot be processed in Nunavut because we have no port to unload it in our communities. If we had at least some facilities in those communities, then we could create opportunities for more training, investment, and employment for these communities. Essential infrastructure could really help our development.

We have worked well with Nunavut Tunngavik Inc.; I have always pushed my own government to go beyond the commitments of the Nunavut Land Claims Agreement, because the more we further assist Inuit, the more our territory catches up to the rest of the Canadian population. In wildlife management, we made sure Inuit were involved in the decision-making process. In education, I made sure that there was money for Inuit education, and for students wanting to pursue post-secondary education. Even though it wasn't our responsibility, we said we'll do it anyway. We were trying to convince the federal government to invest more money in Inuit education, but we still have not seen that happening yet. We went beyond benefits from territorial parks, to show the federal government how it should be done. We went beyond the requirements and expanded projects making sure that we can assist these communities with additional benefits. In partnership with NTI, we put in place the Nunavummi Nangminiqaqtunik

Paul Okalik with his family. From left to right first row: Granddaughter Brynn, Daughter Béatrice, me. Back row: daughter Shasta and son Jordan.

Ikajuuti (NNI), to implement Article 24 of the Nunavut Land Claims Agreement, and tried pushing it beyond the commitments, and made it stronger.[12] We showed the federal government that if you work in true partnership, you avoid a lot of problems, and you create positive opportunities for fellow Canadians. So that's how we tried to push a showcase partnership for the rest of the country. It has helped, but as a territorial government, you only have a limited pot of money that you can use, so it would be nice to have a national partner that can also contribute.

It's a general commitment of the Nunavut Land Claims Agreement to have a government public service that is representative of the population. We honour this spirit of the land claims agreement, and we have created a priority of hiring Inuit, providing additional help for Inuit, but it would be nice to have a national partner to get us further. Nunavut Tunngavik Inc. has taken the federal government to court on this issue.[13] The federal government has tried to include us, the Government of Nunavut, as a third party to the lawsuit. So, even though the Government of Nunavut did not sign the land claims agreement between Inuit and the federal government, we're a partner where we have jurisdiction. In terms of educating Inuit, we do it at the elementary level, but beyond that, the federal government should be supporting Inuit education. The treaty also requires the national government to provide the same benefits and services to Inuit, as they do to the national aboriginal citizens in the country. So the treaty did not move the responsibility of aboriginal issues to the territorial government. The national Inuit issues are still a federal responsibility. I understand why NTI is suing the federal government to have them honour their side of the agreement.

The Nunavut Annual Summer Festival held in front of the Nakasuk Primary School, July 9, 2007. (Photo: Michel Albert)

CHAPTER 10

We Used to Deal with Problems Right Away, and Move On

When there was tension in our traditional camp, the community would try to resolve the problem as quickly and efficiently as possible, so that it would not affect the day-to-day affairs of the family, and of the whole camp; that was very healthy. You didn't have to carry the burden, and be a negative influence on the community. They would deal with the problem quickly, right there, and it would be done; they would move on, and focus on surviving, because they relied on very basic things to survive. But in Canada, the criminal code sets out how these problems are dealt with. First, you're charged and then you have to wait for the next court appearance date, which could be anywhere from six months to a year later. While you're waiting, your whole life is stuck. The problem is there; the case is not being dealt with right away. It could be just a family issue, and it's not being dealt with, because the criminal court prevents you from communicating with the other party, in some cases. So there's no resolution.

Then the court comes in town. There are probably more studies needing to be done; six months later, we'll put you off for another three months or six months, for the lawyers to prepare paperwork. So it could be a year or two years before this case finally can be dealt with! But then, it's not even dealt with, because the guy just ends up in jail. He may have committed suicide at this point, as well. Under the Canadian criminal code those things happen, because of not being able to resolve the case faster and move on.

With our Inuit conflict resolution system, we dealt with problems right away, and move on. We heal, and move on! The Canadian justice system fractures how we used to deal with our problems in the past and how we can still resolve them today. Our system is still used for non-criminal matters. Non-criminal matters are still dealt with in this way, by our elders and family members. If there's tension amongst the family, senior members assist the family in relieving the stress and moving on. I carried a lot of anger as a young man, and I was able to heal with the help of senior members of my family, which let me relieve myself of those burdens, and focus on a more positive life. So it works, but in a lot of cases we're prevented from using our old ways by the criminal code.

I even offered the Federal Minister of Justice to use Nunavut as a pilot project to resolve some of these justice issues outside of the criminal code. The criminal code prohibits you from dealing with some of these matters in a more traditional way. Justice circles assist in healing. But while you wait for your court appearance date, you try to focus on how to move on, but you just think of that day when the judge will decide for you what the outcome will be.

I work with traditional Inuit knowledge. If I have an issue with one of my colleagues, I deal with my colleague directly, and resolve the problem that way, as opposed to using any other means. The first step is to work it out as individuals, and move on. That's my preferred route, and that's what I use. That's what I know, and that's what I've learned, to avoid any other potential problems. One of the things I am working on is looking at our Correction Act, to make sure that we offer more traditional means of healing at the incarceration facility, so that inmates become healthy members of their community when they leave the facility and move on, with a healthier life.[1] Let's focus on that, instead of just focusing on putting them in jail. Let's find a way to move past that point, wherever possible.

This is how I lost my brother, because he had issues with the law. If we can find a way to intervene, and resolve some of these issues, it would be a lot healthier for the individuals, the families and the communities. In my travels so far, I have seen some justice circles that are assuming more work, some cases being diverted to them by the courts, so it definitely helps in terms of dealing with it locally and in a more appropriate way. It's happening, but we need to make it more common, for us to move on and hence reduce the caseload for the courts, and the burden on our corrections system. If we can avoid putting people in jail, and provide them with healthier options, I think we can turn the corner.

Some healthy things are happening. When a woman is working for a salary, the man can be financially supported for his hunting. The woman can provide gas and ammunition to the spouse, allowing him to go hunting. There's no more market for pelts, there's no more commercial income to assist hunters in gathering food for the family on the land. When you're out hunting as a man, you're busy, and you're not only feeding your family, you're feeding your extended family, which may also need country food. That is a very healthy situation. The men need to be able to do that; but they need the skills. When you're out there on the land, you're healing, and you let go of any negative thoughts you may have, because you're focused on what you're doing. I see this happening in some families, and it has helped in that way.

I like going to the river, because that river flows from my forefathers' land, where all my ancestors used to go. So I go there, and heal, and take the time, and focus, and it really helps me. So, it's each individual, but I know it definitely helps a person to go back to the land. It is now part of the correctional programs in some ways, so it definitely helps. Some schools use that too. When the fur prices were good, you saw a lot less social strain in the communities. Hunters feed their family and they serve their community. It makes them feel good and proud. When you can't do that, it adds to the stress.

Mental health is something we will have to focus on, to tackle some of our deep challenges today, such as suicide and becoming healthier people. It's a very challenging issue, because you can't see it, you can only see the indicators of mental health issues. It is largely very individualistic as a problem, because you can't really diagnose it unless the person is seeking help, or the family member recognizes that the individual needs help. It's not like you have a broken bone and you need treatment. It's a real challenge for our government.

When I had my first meeting with Stephen Harper, before he became Prime Minister, he was asking me, "How come Inuit have so many children? And they have all of these housing problems?" The way I look at it is: I'm educated, I'm working, and I'm proud of that, and I'm supporting my family. But I will not add to the stress in my own family by making more kids, for example, because I can only afford so much, to support myself and my family. But if people don't have the education, how can they be responsible for their well-being? They don't have a job, they don't have income, and they end up being dependent on the state, for welfare. I told him, "We can focus on educating the Inuit population to be able to sustain themselves by getting jobs." We all realize that we can't just keep making children, for example, because we can only earn so much, and afford to raise only a number of children. So I was trying to educate him on trying to focus on investing in education for Inuit and aboriginal people. He seemed to understand, but his government never really addressed the problem. When you have education, you can afford to invest in a home, which reduces the burden on the state, because you want to own your own home, not be dependent on the state to give you a certain size house or apartment. That's the freedom you get as an educated person. Getting the best education possible, you can get maybe a government apartment to start with, and then move on from there. The more education you have, the more opportunities you create for yourself. I always stress that with the students that I see. Our government will help them, and pay for their expenses if they choose to go to university or college. That's a benefit Nunavummiut have for living in our territory.

Mark Tungilik is positioned to harpoon a seal at a breathing hole on the sea ice at Naujaat/Repulse Bay, Nunavut, in November 1973. (Photo: Ludger Müller-Wille)

CHAPTER 11

Still Frozen in Time!

I'd like to see more progress in Nunavut. That's my hope. We have made progress, but I see continuing struggles for our social and economic well-being here in our territory; I find it an ongoing challenge. I wish we could do more in investing in education and in ways to improve our communities. Sure, it's nice to build an airport, but does that get us to where we want to go?[1] I'm not sure. It is a good thing for people who travel once in a while, but it doesn't affect the day-to-day lives of our communities as much as having a good education and a rewarding job, for example. As a government, we need to focus on the most important priorities.

The airport upgrading project in Iqaluit has basically frozen any other capital projects for the territory for many years. It was a decision made by the previous Aariak government, so we have to live with it. The Government of Nunavut built a terminal and a garage. They resurfaced the airstrip but we have done that now and again. We resurfaced it in 2007-2008 and it never cost that much. This airport project cost four hundred million dollars plus! We'll pay for it for the next thirty years.

Greenland leads the way in the Inuit world, in terms of advancing in the modern era. In the current environment that we live in, they're way ahead of us in terms of socioeconomic issues and the economy, and how they deal with their challenges. They have a university, for example. With 400 million, we could have created a nice university among other things! We could have done a lot of good things; it's unfortunate. *C'est la vie!* What can you do? You make do with what you have. The federal government is investing $72.8 million in that airport project, and the balance will be paid by the government of Nunavut.[2]

We have to have a balance. We want our citizens to have the opportunity to assume roles and responsibilities in the Canadian society. So they need to be able to speak English or French for them to advance in a national context. But as an Inuk, I'm always an Inuk first. We were here before Canada. Other Inuit have said we're Canadian First.[3] Well, what has Canada done for me? How have they treated me? This is the question I am asking. We need to advance with some federal help to get there, and until that day comes, and we become equal with the rest of the country, I'm not overly proud of being Canadian. I do support my country, when it comes to Olympics or whatever, yes, I will always support my country. But we need to go past the point of just leaving us behind constantly as a people, and allow the North to prosper like the rest of the country. That's my view, and I'm very pleased with my fellow Inuit in Greenland, because they've been allowed to do that by Denmark. They live in a state economy, where everything is pretty much governed by the state. We live in a different economy here, but I believe we can do a bit of both, where the state has a role in improving the standing of the Inuit communities, while allowing the private sector to prosper, with Inuit involved in the long run as well. Right now, there's not a lot of Inuit in the business sector. It's all pretty much fly-in contractors who come to our communities, make money, and move on. It will be nice to see Inuit advance in that area too, and benefit from our government contracts. It will be nice to see some change.

The arctic co-operative movement has done well in the small communities. They have assisted many Inuit in their community. But here in Iqaluit, for example, you can't really have an Inuit co-op. Co-op membership is open to everybody; look at the population here. Inuit aren't a majority anymore in Iqaluit. I believe we're right on the limit. It would not be a solely Inuit community that would run the co-op here. In the small communities, absolutely, it's nice to see more Inuit involved in the co-ops and in the employment opportunities that are created by the co-ops.

Look at the American investments in Alaska, for example, how they built a road for that state; they invested, and Alaska prospered. And where are we in Canada? Can you show me a map in the world where there's two million square kilometres of territory, and you can't get to it by road? It's the only part of the world being that isolated! That's where we are. It's astonishing to see this situation when at the same time Canada boasts that we're First World, and an energy superpower. It's a challenge. If I look at the history of our country, the national government built railroads and infrastructure to develop the remote regions and allow the citizens to prosper. I'm waiting for that day to come for Nunavut; we're still frozen in time!

We've been pressing our national government to allow us to contribute to our sovereignty. We had a constant presence, and an historical use of the land in the Arctic. We're always used for the benefit of our country for asserting Canadian sovereignty over our traditional land, but at the same time we have to catch up to the rest of the world, support those communities, and assert our presence in the modern world. And we're far from being there. It's nice to build icebreakers and those things, but where are they going to refuel?[4] Where are they going to land their boats in our territory, if they have problems? It's still under development, but it's not there. How are these decisions going to benefit our communities that are living there permanently? We see a total absence of investment in the people by the federal government. How will that allow us to grow and prosper like the rest of the country? The federal government priorities are misguided in that way. The ships are being built down South; is that supporting the North in any way, shape, or form? They'll be used up here, but have they trained any of us to take part in those patrol operations? I have not seen any. I see a total lack of investment in the people that way, in terms of allowing us to take part and support our sovereignty. Prime Minister Harper said nice words about the North, and came to Nunavut for military exercises, but when those exercises were over, what are we left with? Not much!

I saw the infrastructure of the Canadian High Arctic Research Station being built in Cambridge Bay; that will require energy, and our Cambridge Bay power plant is not ready for that kind of facility.[5] So, is the national government going to contribute to building up the power needs for that hamlet expansion? I don't know. I haven't seen it. It's good to see investment, but we have to be well prepared to accommodate the new infrastructures.

The way it's going nowadays in Nunavut, if we continue to neglect, as the national government does by not providing any support for educating the Inuit population, we'll need to import more skilled workers from elsewhere. So, yes, there's definitely a possibility that the balance of the population could change in Nunavut, as long as the national government continues to allow Inuit to suffer and others to prosper, in our own homeland. There is a real probability for Inuit to become a minority in Nunavut. Market forces will dictate what events will occur.

We put in provisions in the Nunavut Land Claims Agreement, where if there was going to be any activity on Inuit land-mining activity or other activity, that they would have to negotiate a contract with Inuit for employment, training, and other benefits. So that's been at play on Baffin Island. There's a requirement to train the work force. It definitely helps Inuit get employment opportunities in those projects. Where projects are off Inuit land, we saw opportunity as a government, when I was leading the government, to get involved. The mining companies wanted some incentives and lobbied the government for removing the territorial tax on fuel, and I said, "Look, if we're going to do that, I'd like to see tangible benefits coming to the community." So I insisted that they would have to negotiate with the communities impacted, for training and employment opportunities. And that's what occurred outside of Baker Lake. So we've tried to cover where the land claims could not meet some of the needs in another area as a government, to allow benefits to flow to the communities.

Mining companies are contributing to training our workforce, but only for some really immediate, basic needs—such as heavy equipment operators, labour, and those things. I'd like to see Inuit geologists, Inuit management of mines, which are the kind of things I'd like to see in the long run. You need more than those benefit agreements with mining companies for Inuit to prosper even further. We see the value of training as well; we put in a trade school in Rankin Inlet, to prepare for the mining opportunities, so that we can take on the jobs. When you are a heavy crane operator, you can transfer that skill to a hamlet, where you can operate heavy equipment. As a mechanic, you can work in a mine, and then when that mine shuts down you can work in a hamlet garage. So those are transferable skills that can continue once the mine is concluded. Such training programs will be beneficial in the long run for our territory.

We have the Baffin Land Iron Mines that is so rich in ore you don't really need to melt it. So I don't see a lot of environmental impact happening in that area. Diamond development is just about separating rock, so there's no real chemicals used. There are benefits from these types of mines, in that you don't really contaminate the environment so much. Yes, there will be a hole in the ground, but there's usually a requirement to restore the site whenever the project is concluded. I don't recall the use of harsh chemicals being introduced in Baker Lake, so I think they're using a different technology. It's surrounded by lakes, so I think they're doing whatever they need to do without introducing poisons that are toxic to the environment.

We don't have the money to get involved in any real mining activity. And we don't have control over the resources—that rests with the federal government. So we don't really have any tools to push any developer and attach our conditions to their projects, other than the tools that we have been using through our tax system, or the Inuit Land Claims Agreement. That's where we are different from the provinces. We wouldn't have the money to invest in anything anyway, and really, do we really want to get involved in mines?

CHAPTER 12

Doing My Part to Contribute to Nunavut

We now have twenty-two members at the Legislative Assembly. That's a little much for consensus-based decision-making, so I think there will be a need in the long run to have a party system. Our communities are growing, and they deserve some way of getting their issues addressed. A party system allows for commitments to be made on the outset of an election, and the party system pushes things through. Some people may not agree, but look at the state of our affairs today. We may need a party system to push things along, to make things happen. Consensus is nice; that was our preferred route. But a party platform is a far more effective tool to make things happen. I've thought about it. Look at the numbers today. We have more members in our assembly now, and it's not always possible to arrive at a consensus.[1] In the future, our constituents deserve a clear mandate from politicians. The cabinet system would not change, either a party system or not. It's an ongoing requirement that we work together and set the agenda, and make things happen. But for us to continue on, we need ongoing support from the rest of caucus. I look at the party systems in Greenland and Yukon, and they're getting things done. It is true that Greenland continues to struggle with minority governments, but they find ways to fulfill their agenda. It's a system that works normally, and makes things happen, either way, and we need to have a discussion, I believe, with the current social environment that we're operating under. It's nice to have a long-term view, but to get there, you need to do a number of things. What do you have at your disposal, and how do you take advantage of it? We have to study it, and see how we can make it work and benefit our territory as much as possible.

Our oil and gas supply system is unfortunate; we're paying a heavy price, because we can only buy it once a year. Sometimes we benefit, when the prices are low in the summer, and then they go up in the winter; we're protected that way, but the prices were high in the spring and summer when we bought this batch; those are some things that we tackle in our system. That's what we live with.

For here, in Iqaluit, I believe a number of companies are looking at alternative energy sources such as tidal power; we have the largest tidal power potential, next to the Bay of Fundy, in the country. There's potential to use tidal power. It comes and goes four times a day, and there's energy generated by that, regardless of the season. We have looked into hydro power, but it's something that probably will not happen for a while, because it's a major investment, and our government doesn't have any money to invest. But some private companies are looking at tidal power as an alternative source of energy in Iqaluit. If we look at the central part of our territory, there's lots of wind, so there's potential for wind power there, but the technology is not there yet to provide power in cold weather. I know that they're working on it in the NWT, to supply electricity to the mines. The technology is slowly catching up to what we might need in the central part of our territory, where there's enough wind.

We don't have any real desire to invest in nuclear energy. We don't have the technical knowledge up here, to begin with. It could probably operate, but I don't think we want to go there. There have been discussions for quite some time about getting a transmission line from Manitoba to the Kivalliq region, as a way of reducing energy costs and relying on better energy. That would require federal help, and I don't know if they would move on that one. As well for now, maybe a winter road only is a possibility for supporting a transmission line. In Manitoba, they pay three cents the kilowatt-hour, and in those Kivalliq communities, on average, it's about eighty cents per kilowatt-hour. Look at the amount of savings that could incur for our government in public housing, for example. We pay for all that energy in our offices; the costs could go down for businesses as well. There's a real potential.

I would hope that it's still on the federal agenda, but as a government we put in a modest request for a winter road and transmission line to the federal government, for the time being. We could perhaps turn that into an all-weather road in the long run. It would primarily come from Churchill, Manitoba, connected to the South by railroad, which is the closest major point to Nunavut.

I see more Inuit going to law school in southern Canada. I see Inuit who are trying to get themselves off the ground. They're trying to get themselves educated so that they can take on some of the jobs. What really encourages me is that they're trying. And we need to be there, to help them in the long run. I am committed to the Akitsiraq Law School Program, and I did whatever I could to make it happen again. I think we will see the day when we will have our own law school, but as to when, I can't answer right now.

I have some good memories of working with very good people; not just in Nunavut, but outside, like Premier Stephen Kafkwi of the Northwest Territories; he was like a brother to me.[2] We still stay in touch, and whenever we connect, we're like brothers catching up on anything that's happening in our lives. His name, by the way, is Rabbit Head, and my name is Rabbit, so we pretend to be brothers in that way. I worked well with Dennis Fentie of the Yukon.[3] We did some good things together. Even though he was from a different party, it didn't matter. It's the issues that matter to us, when we're leaders of a government. Like on devolution, we've always supported each other, and I recall putting it on the national agenda, and Yukon benefited by getting an agreement with the Federal government on devolution. From there, it advanced to the Northwest Territories, and they got a devolution agreement not too long ago. Nunavut is the last one yet. That day will come, I'm sure.

I'm committed to my term, and doing what I can to assist my territory. The people of Nunavut spoke, when I tried running in the federal election, and I listened to them. So I'm doing my part to contribute where I can, and doing my best to serve my constituents and my territory. I'm quite content, doing what I'm doing now, and I will continue to serve my territory in whatever capacity they choose me to do so. I'm using my education, my knowledge, to the maximum amount I can, to benefit my territory, and I'm quite pleased with that.

I'm Out!

Stephen Harper unleashed the federal campaign of 2015 very early to disallow any other party activity leading up to the campaign. That made it a very long campaign. I was very actively involved with the Nunavut Liberal Party executive trying to recruit a candidate because the party was the strongest opposition to the Conservatives in our riding. I interviewed numerous good individuals but unfortunately we were not able to select a candidate on time for the campaign. Meanwhile, the national office of the Liberal Party in Ottawa had already received an application from a Nunavut candidate. They decided that we had to go with this candidate, who was Mr. Hunter Tootoo. Consequently, we did everything we could to get him elected. Hunter Tootoo had been previously a New Democratic Party candidate who eventually supported the Conservative Party in the 2011 election! I thought that I had to support whatever worked for the Liberal Party in our riding. I went door to door. I was interviewed on CBC radio with Mr. Tootoo and I talked to anybody I could to support Mr. Tootoo.

I even read a newspaper in a public assembly during the Iqaluit electoral debate to mimic Leona Aglukkaq and protest the silent treatment of Inuit and Nunavut by the Conservative government and how much they cared for our territory and its people.[1] All this worked very well and she lost and got a third place out of four candidates. We were able to get Mr. Tootoo elected and the best day was when he was sworn in to cabinet opening new opportunities for our territory with a government that strongly claimed to be progressive. That was a very good day for us! But unfortunately Hunter Tootoo had his own personal issues and it didn't work out for him in Ottawa and it hasn't worked out for our territory very well since then.

I must say that I am not all happy with our current Liberal government and with the decisions they are making as well. They were willing to move along aboriginal issues, something that would definitively help Nunavut, like implementing the Truth and Reconciliation Commission's report, honouring treaties with aboriginal peoples, dealing with aboriginal peoples on a nation-to-nation relationship, allowing the National Inquiry into Missing and Murdered Indigenous Women. Those issues were what we were expecting to see addressed by this new Liberal government. That is what made me a stronger Liberal during the electoral campaign, and I even hosted Mr. Trudeau and emceed the reception during his visit to Nunavut. We were looking forward to real changes for Nunavut and it hasn't worked out that way.

We are still waiting for the government to honour our treaty rights on gun control for example; according to our Nunavut Land Claims Agreement which is basically a treaty, Inuit don't need any license or papers to exercise our right to hunt. But the requirement is still in place and Inuit need a paper to buy a gun and ammunitions. On the campaign trail, the Prime Minister said that his government would honour treaties; Nunavut Inuit has a modern-day treaty still waiting to be honoured. We are in year three of the Trudeau government and hopefully they will come around with a decision but we are still waiting. Since the election, the federal government has cut back on health care funding. They invested in mental health and yes, we badly need that, but the money they gave us won't have much of an impact for the territory as a whole. It is something that needs to be addressed and focused on to pass where we are at today. I was hoping for a real Nunavut partner with the new Liberal government and it has not worked out that way.

Inuit also have been passed up in serving on the National Inquiry into Missing and Murdered Indigenous Women. Even if Trudeau promoted a nation-to-nation relationship with indigenous peoples, Inuit are still treated as a sub-form of human beings. On the National Inquiry into Missing and Murdered Indigenous Women we didn't get an Inuk commissioner; that was a real disappointment! We still are waiting for the nation-to-nation approach.

The resignation of Hunter Tootoo from the cabinet and the ruling party is a hindrance for Nunavut. How do you get around that? We have only one Member of Parliament for the entire territory. Now the seat is pretty much vacant. Hunter Tootoo is not part of the government; he is not part of a caucus or a party to voice our challenges.

I met with Mr. Tootoo and explained that these had to be addressed and that he was not of any valid help besides facilitating passport procedures, because he is only an independent Member of Parliament. He has no caucus to support his effort. It is rather frustrating. I don't envy his position.

We still wait to work with the federal government. My good acquaintance for now is Larry Bagnell from Yukon who is a Liberal Member of Parliament. I try to work with him and he is trying to help us within the northern caucus. I appreciate his openness and willingness to help us. I continue to express my disappointment to the Prime Minister's Office that there is still no minister from the North in the current government. Harper did better. He had a northern Member of Parliament part of his cabinet. Right now there is no minister from the North, not even a parliamentary secretary from the North. Trudeau is not helping in having our part of the country represented in the decision-making inner circle.

Making a unilateral decision on banning oil and gas development without talking to anyone in the North is a concept that we left behind long ago![2] You have to talk to the people who are the most impacted at least. We are expecting consultation at least. We expect a better treatment. That is a Harper way of governing. That is how the Trudeau government is making decisions and it is not a good way. I hope they will change their way of governing and move forward to a nation-to-nation relationship with Inuit.

We are not alone. The Northwest Territories have expressed their disappointment. They have a Liberal Member of Parliament there too, Michael McLeod. But they don't seem to count. I hope the Prime Minister will soon consider a minister coming from the North. Madame Carolyn Ann Bennett is definitely not doing it out of Toronto. She is the Minister of the Department of Indigenous and Northern Affairs Canada.[3] We need somebody who can represent northern constituencies in the cabinet. We have at least two Members of Parliament in there from the North still. The downfall of Hunter Tootoo's political career within the current Liberal government is a real disappointment for all of us.

Negotiation on devolution is still happening, but considering all the deals that our current Nunavut political leaders have struck, I'm hopeful that we won't have an agreement in time until the next Nunavut government is in place. I look at the deal the former Nunavut Premier, the Honourable Peter Taptuna, struck on the airport terminal in Iqaluit when he was the minister responsible in the Eva Aariak government. As the Minister of Economic Development and Transportation, he negotiated the contracts. It is very expensive for a terminal where you only spend an hour once in a while waiting for a plane. We're stuck with this humongous bill for years to come. I also look at the deal he struck for displaying our art at the Winnipeg Art Gallery; we are paying half a million dollars a year for it! To exhibit our art! This was very disappointing[*].

He pushed on an agreement with the federal government to implement the Inuit employment provisions of the land claims, without any federal funding channelled to our government. We have to beg other governments and organizations to try to get money for Inuit training in our government. I don't see a lot of hope for a real good agreement for our territory under the current administration because this Premier is so one-sided all the time. He always seems to work for the other side! He is not a very good negotiator.

My role in cabinet was to ensure that we support those in need. Primarily, those who have issues with addiction to alcohol and drugs. That was my portfolio as the Minister of Health, and that was my role. Having lived through that experience, and having benefited from the support I got in treatment centres and other programs, I wanted to offer the

---

[*] These remarks were written down before the territorial election on October 30, 2017 when Paul Quassa was elected Premier of Nunavut.

same services for our Nunavut population. I laid the foundation to have local support in each community for those in need before opening a treatment facility. Once they went to the treatment centre and they go back home, they need support. Otherwise they go back to the same routine and they have to move away from that. That was the direction I had given to my department. We were investing.

We had the Minister of Finance who really was keen on opening a beer and wine store. But we needed at least a treatment centre and support for those in need before we do that! All it would do, it would increase the supply for those who really need help. To say that we would displace bootleggers was unrealistic because well, to this day it is not happening. Once they used up their supply from the liquor store they go back to their bootleggers whenever they need it. That argument didn't fly with me because I have been there before. I attended their consultation in Iqaluit where every elder in the community spoke and said, "No, we don't want it right now!" Even their objections were never considered. I looked into the debate that occurred to making change to the Liquor Act for example. Minister Peterson said, "We will consult with the folks of communities close to the proximity of any liquor store." I am still waiting for those consultations to happen. Those debates are in Hansard, so you can look at the commitments that he made and that he didn't honour. I expressed my concerns in cabinet and said that I cannot agree with a government that would do this. I went to the Premier's office and said that I cannot be a part of this government if this is allowed to happen. He kept it on the agenda and let it happen. So I said, "Okay, I can't be a part of this decision." And I let all of my cabinet colleagues know, "I'm out!"

This was my major issue of disagreement with the government. Prior to that, I did what I could to help out and serve as a minister. I did a lot of work during my short two and a half years in the government. I was placed in the most challenging portfolios and I did what I could. Nobody knew what to do with the Power Corporation for example, which was scandal-ridden when we formed the government. I was given the file and I got rid of the management that was causing troubles for new employees, and they never made any more headlines. The next one was the Department of Health, which was challenged with a lot of difficulties in terms of preventable deaths, of general care, and babies' deaths for example. I managed it; we organized consultations and accepted all recommendations that we put in place. I made all those decisions happen in the government. We don't see a lot of controversies there now. We did a lot of hard work to make sure that we honour those who deserved that type of treatment. We did what we could.

I worked with other ministers. I have been a strong advocate for more education in the territory, like in the case of the law program. We pushed that along. I was the Justice Minister and we made sure that this would happen in 2017. There was a Minister of Finance who made sure it was not happening for a long time. The Law program in the past formed people with critical thinking, and that is what we need in our territory to be able to analyse decisions and move forward. This will allow students to study law with a University of Regina program and pursue a career in law, which we really need in Nunavut. I was part of that decision, and I lobbied hard and worked with my cabinet colleagues to make it happen. So these are good things that we accomplished but at the same time, some issues like the Inuit employment in the government workforce is a very challenging one. I openly continue to support Inuit employees and to push for more training for them regardless of where I am sitting. It never stopped when I was part of cabinet.

Education and training lead to better opportunities for our citizens. When Inuit do well, the whole territory does well. When people are not doing anything, they are not being contributors, they are on welfare, they are doing other things that are not healthy for them or the community. We need to find ways to keep our citizens active. When they are working, they are contributing; they are living healthier lives, mentally and otherwise.

The financial settlement between NTI and Ottawa on Inuit training

Since the financial settlement of $255 million between Nunavut Tunngavik Inc. and Ottawa on Inuit training, the current NTI leaders gave the government of Nunavut only two seats on the seven-member board of the Makigiaqta Inuit Training Corp., without money. So the Government of Nunavut still has to go to Ottawa and say, "Can you give us training money?" As a result that NTI training money is out of the Government of Nunavut control, even though the government is the largest employer in the territory.[4]

I tried to explain to our current leaders that even on training programs in our own government, Inuit are receiving less for training. We are training more non-Inuit for management positions on a per capita basis. You try to lead by doing whatever you can. But when you go to these federal agencies, it is rather disappointing because you have to show first that you are doing whatever you can in your jurisdiction for training your workforce and that you need extra funding, but we even cannot bring that argument.

A charter of rights allows for additional help for those groups who have been disadvantaged or discriminated against in the past, which we are as Inuit. It is any level of government responsibility. Any government has the duty to try to accommodate those specific conditions. But our Nunavut government comes with the argument that "We are a public government." When you look at the training opportunities, it does not go primarily to Inuit; it goes to largely non-Inuit who do not need the additional support that we do need. It is a public government for everybody else except Inuit when it comes to training. When it comes to signage on buildings, a lot of signage is still not in Inuktitut when it is required by our own law! It seems to be a public government for everybody else except Inuit, the only true native inhabitants of the territory. That is something that needs to change.

Photo taken on 16 October 1883 at Ujarasugdjuling in Kangertloaping
Bay by then German anthropologist Franz Boas when arctic sovereignty
was a source of contention. Boas' assistant Wilhelm Weike is on the left;
to their right are their Inuit companions Nachojaschi, Singnar
and Utütiak. (Photo: *American Philosophical Society*)

Nunavut: The Long Road Before – Historical Context
by Louis McComber

The creation of Nunavut was a defining moment in the recent history of Canada. The Government of Canada was writing a new chapter in the saga of the great Northwest. April 1, 1999 was an historical moment. The multiple inaugural events were broadcasted all over the world by international media. It was an opportunity to offer a new national narrative for the centuries of controversial administration of aboriginal peoples in Canada.

A significant turning point in the relationship of Canada with indigenous peoples had occurred in the 1980s. Four First Ministers' conferences on Aboriginal Constitutional Matters failed to reach any clear agreement on a constitutional definition of aboriginal rights, as required by Section 35 of the 1982 Constitution Act.[1]

On a more dramatic note, Canadian military became the focus of international attention when in August 1990 they were called in by the Quebec and Canadian governments to help end the Oka crisis in Kanesatake and Kahnawake, two Mohawk communities located near Montreal. The Kanesatake Mohawks resisted an Oka

municipal council decision to allow a golf course enlarge-
ment in a pine grove on a land dedicated for their usage by
the King of France in 1717.[2] To manifest their solidarity,
the Kahnawake Mohawks swiftly organized a blockade
of the Mercier bridge connecting the south shore highway to Montreal. As some kind of institutional closure to
this crisis, the Royal Commission on Aboriginal Peoples
was set up by the Federal Conservative government. The
Royal Commission, which was held from 1992 through
1996, was an informative opportunity to look back at more
than three hundred years of marginalisation of indigenous peoples, but also a new attempt to clarify the extent
of the aboriginal title in Canada. Does it involve more
than some kind of traditional right to use and profit from
the land? Could it be that the aboriginal title in Canada
entails some forms of aboriginal self-government? The
Royal Commission introduced a radical departure from
the traditional official Canadian discourse in addressing
aboriginal issues in Canada:

> Let us be clear, however. To say that Aboriginal peoples are
> nations is not to say that they are nation-states seeking inde-
> pendence from Canada. They are collectivities with a long
> shared history, a right to govern themselves and, in general,
> a strong desire to do so in partnership with Canada.[3]

In this controversial context in which the liberal repu-
tation of Canada was questioned on international forums
and media on its administration of aboriginal issues, the
creation of Nunavut aimed to establish a public government over a territory where people of Inuit ancestry
represent 85 percent of the population. Since there was
no doubt that a majority of Inuit representatives would
be elected at the Nunavut Legislative Assembly, Inuit
self-government would become a non-issue, especially

with the Nunavut Tunngavik Inc., the political organization representing the Nunavut Inuit, monitoring the
political process.

Inuit self-government was a very dear concept to
Canadian Inuit ever since they first filed their land claims
proposal to the Canadian government in 1975. Their
national representative organization, Inuit Tapirisat
of Canada established in 1971, now called Inuit Tapiriit
Kanatami, had included in their land claims the creation
of a territorial government in which Inuit would be the
majority of the population. Their first 1975 proposal that
implied an ethnic form of government was not considered
by federal negotiators. Negotiations with the federal government began seriously when the Inuit agreed to a public
government.

Paul Okalik got involved in 1985 in the Nunavut Land
Claims Agreement negotiations as a deputy negotiator
and eventually as the Chief Negotiator with the Tunngavik
Federation of Nunavut until the signing of an Agreement
in Principle in 1990.

In the last months of a vulnerable Mulroney government
in 1993, signing the Nunavut Inuit land claims proposal provided some kind of political good news for the Conservative
government.[4] It also provided good news on the constitutional front after the failed attempts by the Conservatives to
modify the 1982 Constitution with the Meech Lake Accord,
which would have allowed Quebec to sign it, followed by the
Charlottetown Accord that was rejected nationally by both
the federal referendum in all provinces other than Quebec
and the Quebec referendum in October of 1992. The core
issue of both accords was the recognition of Quebec as a
distinct society. That didn't go well with many Canadians,
especially with aboriginal peoples who were mostly left

out of the Meech Lake Accord and not convinced by the Charlottetown Accord debates.

Like a rabbit pulled out of a magician's hat, the Nunavut project was an opportunity for Ottawa to show the world that cultural and political diversity were possible within the framework of the 1982 Constitution Act, which Quebec has still not ratified. The Government of Quebec, with the unanimous support of all its political parties, has perceived the 1982 Constitution and especially the Canadian Charter of Rights and Freedoms, based on the protection of individual rights more than collective rights, as a direct threat to its existence as a distinct society and an intrusion in the jurisdiction of the Quebec National Assembly. The demographic components of the new territory of Nunavut could compare on a much smaller scale to the demographic components of the Province of Quebec, where more than 80 percent of the population uses French as their first language spoken at home. It is interesting to recall the comment of Brian Mulroney at the signing ceremony of the Nunavut Land Claims Agreement on May 25, 1993 in Iqaluit, Northwest Territories:

> We are forging a new partnership, a real partnership. Not only between the Government of Canada and the future Government of Nunavut but between aboriginal and non-aboriginal Canadians.[5]

The reengineering of the Canadian narrative on aboriginal issues, and indirectly on the Quebec sovereignty claim, culminated at the inaugural ceremonies in Iqaluit on April 1, 1999. In the newly chosen Capital, Prime Minister Jean Chretien declared:

> Canada is showing the world, once again, how we embrace many peoples and cultures. The new Government of

Nunavut will reflect this diversity, incorporating the best of Inuit traditions and a modern system of open and accountable public government.[6]

The very name of the country given by Jacques Cartier in 1534, Canada, is thought to be of Iroquoian origin, meaning a village, among other interpretations. For centuries, the history of the country revolved around the relationship between fur traders of European origins and the original peoples of the continent. As the Canadian historian Harold Innis pointedly noted in 1930, "We have not yet realized, that the Indian and his culture were fundamental to the growth of Canadian institutions."[7] John Ralston Saul has reactivated this surprising perspective on the history of Canada in recent publications. It is surprising considering the degree of intolerance for non-British cultures among very influential circles such as the Toronto Family Compact or the Clique du Château in Quebec in the nineteenth century, or the popular Canadian branches of the Loyal Order of Orange, and even the Canadian Ku Klux Klan that gained ground in English-speaking Canada at the beginning of the twentieth century. All were devoted to the supremacy of white Anglo-Saxon and Protestant loyalists and the British Crown.[8] [9] Four Prime Ministers of Canada were Orangemen including John A. Macdonald, the father of the Indian Act and of residential schools for aboriginal peoples.[10] [11] [12]

The story of the oppression of aboriginal peoples by federal Indian agents applying department policies is very well documented by different Royal Commissions, the Hawthorn Tremblay Commission (1966-1967), the Royal Commission on Aboriginal Peoples (1996), and the Truth and Reconciliation Commission (2008-2015). The National Inquiry into Missing and Murdered Indigenous Women and Girls (2017-) is shedding light on the dramatic social consequences of such colonial postures on the lives of families and individuals. Colonialist policies over aboriginal affairs are now also strongly documented in the work of many academics and since the seventies by an impressive number of aboriginal intellectuals.

In his intellectual endeavour to reconcile Canada as a great nation, Saul challenges this conservative and basically racist vision of Canada by showcasing the post-1837 rebellion movement of Lafontaine and Baldwin, which led to the responsible government in Upper and Lower Canada in 1848.[13] For Saul, this was the birth of the real inclusive Canada, although for the French Canadian majority it doused any hope of controlling their own political destiny by creating the conditions for them to become forever a minority faced with large waves of English-speaking immigrants. Before the 1870 Métis rebellion, the existence in Canada of a pre-European occupation of the land was not a determining factor in the plans of pre-confederation politicians.

The creation of Nunavut in 1999 then was to provide some kind of historical answer about the real nature of Canada. Can an aboriginal people survive and thrive with its own culture and language in what is described as the Canadian 'mosaic,' thus demonstrating the benevolent nature of the Canadian federation? Can Inuit succeed in creating an Inuit user-friendly government? And a sub-question: can the newly created territory just function as a political jurisdiction with the monumental challenges at hand?

The Danish anthropologist Jens Dahl made an enlightening observation about the creation of Nunavut. He argued that the Greenlandic Inuit have developed a sense of collective identity that is nationalistic, steadily manifesting their political desire for the creation of a political entity independent from Denmark. Alaskan Inupiat people are more community rooted, defining themselves more as American first. Dahl claims that Nunavut Inuit are constructing an in-between identity.[14] Very much community based, Nunavut Inuit are proud to be Canadian, but hope to develop a unified territorial identity that is still under construction. Dahl argues that the fact Greenland is an island far away from Denmark, while Nunavut, except for Baffin Island, is geographically attached to Canada and the continent, may be a factor in the way Canadian Inuit position themselves.[15]

The late Jose Kusugak, a former President of NTI and ITK, summarized this conception of Canadian Inuit identity in a sharp statement: First Canadians, Canadian first!

> Do Inuit see themselves as Inuit first or as Canadians first? I have always thought those two sentiments were one and the same. After all, during our many meetings with Inuit from countries such as Denmark, the United States or Russia, we have always been Canadian Inuit.[16]

For Arctic Inuit, the Canadianization of their homeland took a very different turn from that of the indigenous populations in the South where they were subjected to the Indian Act as of 1876. The Canadian Arctic was first a playfield for the British Navy explorers until 1880, when the Crown ceded the British Islands to Canada. At the same time the British Admiralty conducted expeditions, British, Scottish, and later American whaling vessels were intensely active until the beginning of World War I in 1914, when the resource was completely depleted, but also when whale oil and baleen were abruptly replaced by mineral oil and plastic on international markets.

Obviously Inuit lands were not under pressure from a wave of migrant farmers as was the case in the Canadian West, especially after the construction of the transcontinental railroad (1881-1885) and the Yukon gold rush. European contacts with Inuit were driven by explorers, whalers, and afterward by the Hudson's Bay Company, which intensively traded for fox pelts.

In 1848, the whaling Captain John Parker wrote a memorial to Queen Victoria about the situation in the Cumberland Sound, arguing that the British government should do something to alleviate the suffering and misery of the Cumberland Sound Inuit. Twenty Inuit out of a population of one hundred and seventy had starved to death in the previous summer at Blacklead Island (Niantilik):

> Your Majesty's Memorialist has been deeply impressed, from personal observation, with their miserable lot; and with great humility ventures to suggest that the most effectual method of securing their permanent benefit will be to colonize the western part of Davis' Straits, -making Hogarth Sound (Cumberland Sound) the principal station- in the manner which has for many years been adopted by the Danish Government on the eastern side, where the natives are comparatively happy and where there is no risk of their being subjected to the horrible calamities which those on the western coast have continually to endure.
>
> ... Finally, a reply was drafted, which said, "Sincerely as Lord Grey (the colonial secretary) laments the sufferings and distress of these tribes, it has not been in his power to advise Her Majesty to sanction the formation of any settlement in their neighbourhood, or adopt the other measures suggested in the memorial for their relief."[17]

The British colonial administration's disinterest for the Canadian Arctic population was passed on to Canadian authorities when the Arctic Islands were ceded to Canada in 1880. When the Minister of the Interior and Mines in the liberal government of William Lyon Mackenzie King, Charles Stewart, was informed of Inuit populations being decimated by famines, he proposed an amendment in 1924 to bring the Inuit under the Indian Act, thus confirming the fiduciary role of Ottawa with regard to the Inuit. The former Conservative Prime Minister Arthur Meighen opposed the amendment and it was altered so as not to include Inuit under the Indian Act and thus avoid creating a federal legal obligation to take responsibility for their welfare:

> Meighen objected to Inuit coming under these provisions of the Indian Act. He opposed the proposal to "nurse" them and to make them "wards" of the government as Indians were popularly regarded. In particular, he objected to the government taking "the control and management of the lands and property of the Eskimos in Canada."[18]

The Quebec government launched a successful lawsuit against the federal government in 1939 before the Supreme Court of Canada that forced Ottawa to cover the costs of relief rations distributed to starving Inuit families in Northern Quebec. The judges decided that Eskimos were Indians and should be administered under the Indian Act.[19]

Canada left the fate of the Eskimos in the hands of the greedy uncle, the Hudson's Bay Company. The company developed a network of Arctic trading posts at the end of the whaling era. Most federal government relief would be distributed to Inuit through their trading posts.[20]

A few North West Mounted Police (now the Royal Canadian Mounted Police) stations were established to claim sovereignty for the Canadian government and collect duties from American whalers and Yukon gold diggers who ventured into the Canadian Arctic in the Yukon, at Herschel Island, in Hudson's Bay Roes Welcome Sound, at Cape Fullerton and later at Pond Inlet on Baffin Island.[21] The Liberal government of Sir Wilfrid Laurier launched annual sovereignty patrols. The first was commanded by William Wakeham in 1897 who officially took possession of the Arctic Islands for Canada. It was followed by an expedition commanded by the geographer Albert Peter Low in 1903, and later the many voyages of Captain Joseph Elzéar Bernier beginning in 1905 establishing Canadian sovereignty in the Arctic.[22]

Meanwhile in Greenland, the Danish geographer H. J. Rink (1819-93) had managed to publish a newspaper in Greenlandic, *Kalaallisut*, as early as 1859, called the *Atuagagdliutit*. The capital of Greenland, then Godthab, now Nuuk, was founded in 1728 by a Lutheran missionary, Hans Egede, with the full support of the Kingdom of Denmark. While Canada was sending mainly policemen and missionaries to the North, Greenland had doctors, schools, a trading company, and a newspaper in the vernacular language. That difference in social organization was obvious for any whaling ship mooring at Disco Bay on their trip to Baffin Bay. "In 1910, Greenland's elite founded a nationalist movement with the motto 'forward and upward' and was talking of Greenland as a nation."[23]

In contrast to this Danish style of colonial administration, Keith J. Crowe, a long time bureaucrat of the Department of Indian Affairs and Northern Development, depicts the situation in the Arctic in 1939.

The ceremony of taking possession of the entire Arctic Archipelago in front of Parry's Rock, Winter Harbour, Melville Island, 1 July 1909. Captain Joseph Elzéar Bernier is in the front row surrounded by his officers while a muskox calf is licking his hand. (Bernier Collection, *Master Mariner*)

The police did their best, but they were not trained or equipped to be a whole administration. One well-known writer on the north, Dr. Diamond Jenness, pointed out in one of his books that in 1939 the Canadian government spent $17 on police in the north for every one of the Inuit; Denmark spent nothing, for there were no police in Greenland; and only 41 cents was spent in Alaska. At the same time Canada spent only $12 a head on education, health, and welfare of the Inuit compared to $13 in Alaska and $44 in Greenland. Of Canada's $12, five was paid by Inuit from taxes on the furs they sold.[24][25]

Perhaps nothing better could have been done under the circumstances, but in 1939 Soviet Inuit were piloting aircraft, Alaskan natives were running businesses, and Greenlanders were electing their own people to their own councils. Canadian Indians, Métis, and Inuit of the north in

that year were without a voice in economics, religion, education, laws, or politics. From proud people who rather pitied
the clumsy foreigner they had become bewildered bystand-
ers, an embarrassment to a government that did not know
what to do next.[26]

Before the Second World War, non-Inuit living in the
Arctic were mostly Europeans: Scots working for the
Hudson's Bay Company, British Anglican missionaries
from the London Missionary Society, and French and
Belgian priests from the French Catholic religious order
of the Oblates. Once again, the Royal Canadian Mounted
Police officers represented the main genuine Canadian
presence. From the time the United States entered the
Second World War, American workers and military per-
sonnel became the largest single group of people in the
Canadian Arctic. They built the Alaska Highway and the
Canol pipeline from Norman Wells to Alaska. They built
and managed a string of air bases across the continent to
fly newly manufactured California bombers to England.
These included The Pas, Fort Churchill, Southampton
Island, for the Hudson Bay route; Mingan, Goose Bay, Fort
Chimo (now Kuujuaq), and Frobisher Bay (now Iqaluit)
for the northeast staging route, and Moose Factory,
Richmond Gulf, and Baffin Island for the Central Route.
Twenty-eight airfields and fifty-six weather stations were
built.[27] The Star and Stripes was then flying all over the
Canadian Arctic.

The end of the Second World War didn't stop US military activity in the Canadian North. The confrontation
between the United States and their former allies with
the Soviet Union under Stalin had the world fearing an
apocalyptic atomic war. The confrontation flared up in
1949, when the Soviets blocked the access to Berlin in

Germany to the US Allies. At the same time the US Air Force started planning a radar detection system that would cover the whole continent on the Canadian side of the border. The first line of radars was called the Pinetree line, running approximately along the 50th parallel. That line was rapidly outdated and not really efficient. Another line of 90 radar stations farther north was planned. It ran between Newfoundland and Alaska along the 55th parallel. This technology was also rapidly outdated, and the Royal Canadian Air Force jointly with the US Air Force decided to go ahead with the Distant Early Warning radar system that would run further north, 300 kilometres north of the Arctic Circle. The construction started in 1954 and employed 25,000 workers. The US Air Force covered the cost of construction of the 63 stations scattered between Alaska and Baffin Island. Even Canadian officials had to use US currency when travelling on the American bases, stirring serious questions about the degree of Canadian sovereignty over its Arctic regions.[28] Many Nunavut communities today are located nearby former DEW line stations, such as Broughton Island, Hall Beach, Coral Harbour, or Iqaluit. By 1963, the US Air Force had transferred all their bases and equipment to the Canadian government, which inherited the job of eliminating all the toxic material. The presence of American and Canadian military personnel in the Arctic, and so many construction workers brought attention to the appalling conditions of life of the Inuit.[29]

The government of Canada started waking up to its Arctic population in the 1950s, during the Cold War, when mostly US Air Force personnel were shocked by the appalling living conditions of Canadian Eskimos, as they were called at the time. In Canada, Farley Mowat's

book *People of the Deer* (1953) and *The Desperate People*
(1959), along with the German photographer Richard
Harrington's *The Face of the Arctic* documented the starvation of Padleimiut and shook up both a national and
international audience as well as the Liberal Government
of Louis St-Laurent. That was when things started to
move in the Canadian Arctic. Settlements were established, federal schools and basic housing were developed,
small businesses were supported, especially the emerging co-operative movement which was facilitated by the
financial support of the Eskimo Loan Fund, an economic
development initiative first created in 1953 to help the
High Arctic relocated families. An annual Canadian Arctic
patrol was launched in 1950 sailing on a newly built vessel, the *CGS C.D. Howe*. The vessel became infamously
known for plucking from their communities many family members struggling with infectious diseases such as
tuberculosis and taking them down to southern sanato-
riums and hospitals. Many of these patients never made
it back home. The ship is also known for having been used
to relocate families from Inukjuak in Nunavik to the High
Arctic in 1953, for the purpose of asserting the sovereignty
of Canada on these contested remote regions.[30]

The recent political developments in the three Canadian Northern territories are a continuation of a long saga
of marginalisation of indigenous peoples that shaped the
core of Canadian history. They are stories of encounters
between different peoples, different cultures, with some
being organized as industrial empires and others being
only recently introduced to trade and money, Christianity,
literacy, and European infectious diseases. The pre-
European North American world had no clear notion of
fee simple property, of social classes, of some institution-

The hospital boat *CGS C.D. Howe* became infamously known for plucking family members with infectious diseases from their communities
and taking them south. (Photo: Canada. Dept. of Transport/Library
and Archives Canada)

alized forms of writing. These phenomena started emerging in much more populated societies with a higher level
of complexity such as the Quechua, the Maya, or Toltec
kingdoms of Central and South America, brutally inter-
rupted by Spanish Conquistadors who pillaged the continent and exterminated millions of human beings. This
is called colonialism, European countries competing
militarily with each other for accessing wealth in foreign
territories. Humanitarian concerns for local populations
had little place in that colonial world.

In the United States, the military removal and relocation of American Indians were conducted throughout the
nineteenth century under the Removal Act of 1830 passed
under the presidency of Andrew Jackson, and later by the
multiple Indian Appropriations Acts (1851-1871-1885...)
allowing violent repression of resisting tribes such as the

Muscogee/Creeks, the Comanche, the Apache, Sioux, Cheyenne, Navaho, the Nez Percé... The relocation of the Cherokees, the educated Indians, to the state of Oklahoma left thousands dead on the infamous Trail of Tears of 1838-1839. These appalling massacres were conducted – and legitimized – under what has come to be known as the United States' Manifest Destiny.

In Canada, the current federal police, the Royal Canadian Mounted Police, was created in 1873 as a detachment of rangers to pacify the Northwest and most especially the Red River Valley where the Métis had attempted to establish a provisional government led by Louis Riel in 1870. Then it was called the Northwest Mounted Police. In Batoche, Saskatchewan, in 1885, regiments of the Canadian military equipped with canons and machine guns defeated the Métis commanded by Louis Riel and Gabriel Dumont in May, and the Cree commanded by Big Bear in July. The relocation of Indian tribes on reserves under a series of numbered treaties opened up the West to the Transcontinental Railroad (1881-1885). Canadians like to think that the removal of indigenous peoples on this side of the border was more elegant than in United States. That is not the understanding of the health researcher James William Daschuk. In his book *Clearing the Plains: Disease, Politics of Starvation, and the Loss of Aboriginal Life,* he demonstrates that the John A. McDonald Conservative government widely made use of starvation to pressure plains tribes to move onto reservations.[31]

> The government was well aware of the delicate balance between its policy of starving holdouts into submission and onto reserves and the risk of scandal from widespread death from hunger.[32]

The famine caused by repeated cuts in funding of Indian administration combined with infectious diseases, such as smallpox and tuberculosis, decimated thousands of Canadian aboriginal people who had no local health facilities to fight these epidemics. A disturbing document published in 1922 qualifies this organized negligence as a "national crime." It is written by Henderson Peter Bryce M.A., M.D., Medical Inspector of the Interior and of Indian Affairs. Dr. Bryce reports that 24 percent of indigenous children attending residential schools nationwide never went back home. Most died of infectious diseases.

> It (the report) contained a brief history of the origin of the Indian Schools, of the sanitary condition of the schools and statistics of the health of the pupils, during the 15 years of their existence. Regarding the health of the pupils, the report states that 24 per cent, of all the pupils which had been in the schools were known to be dead, while of one school on the File Hills reserve, which gave a complete return to date, 75 per cent, were dead at the end of the 16 years since the school opened.[33]

At the time Dr. Bryce was writing his report there were no medical facilities all across the Canadian Arctic. The first hospital was built by the Anglican mission in 1926 in Aklavik in the Mackenzie Delta. The Catholic mission followed suit the next year also in Aklavik. An Anglican hospital was later built in Pangnirtung in the Eastern Arctic in 1928, and a Catholic hospital was built in Chesterfield Inlet, Igluligaarjuk, in the northern Hudson Bay area in 1929.[34]

Here is how Abraham Okpik, an Inupiat born in the Mackenzie Delta, describes the plight of Inupiat and Inuit stricken by infectious diseases:

My parents were on an island somewhere with their parents when a whaling ship landed at Atkinson Point, just east of today Tuktoyaktuk and Kittigazuit. ... after they left, the whole settlement died. ... They didn't have any medicine to combat it, so you were lucky if you survived.[35]

Keith Crowe estimated that in 1910 only 130 Mackenzie Delta Inuit survived the whaling era out of a population of approximately 2,000. The community of Kittigazuit was completely wiped out by infectious diseases brought by the whalers.[36] Because of the abundance of sea mammals, it was the most populated gathering place of the Arctic with a semi-sedentary population of approximately a thousand people. Could the word genocide apply to qualify the negligence of the Canadian authorities to not provide adequate medical services or minimal services across the Arctic?[37]

The Government of Canada, panicked by the proliferation of cases of tuberculosis among the Inuit population when southern Canada had strongly reduced its occurrence, decided to treat the Inuit down South rather than develop medical facilities in the Arctic.

Rather than constructing treatment facilities in northern communities, the government sent large numbers of Inuit to sanatoria and hospitals in southern Canada for care. In 1956, 10% of the Inuit population was receiving medical treatment, mainly for tuberculosis, in southern Canadian hospitals. Between 1953 and 1964, 4,836 Inuit in the NWT were hospitalized, and 75% to 80% of them were sent to sanatoria in southern Canada. Many missionaries and civil servants in the North were critical of this action, based on the trauma that separation caused Inuit families.[38]

The aftermath of the Second World War saw the rise of a multitude of national revolutionary movements, breaking apart colonial empires and most importantly the belief of absolute superiority of a 'human race' over others. The United Nations agreed on the Universal declaration of Human Rights proclaimed in 1948. It was clearly heralding a new era of relationships between so many diverse peoples on the planet. But what about indigenous peoples? Could the words of the declaration apply to them?

Article 1.
All human beings are born free and equal in dignity and rights. They are endowed with reason and conscience and should act towards one another in a spirit of brotherhood.

Article 2.
Everyone is entitled to all the rights and freedoms set forth in this Declaration, without distinction of any kind, such as race, colour, sex, language, religion, political or other opinion, national or social origin, property, birth or other status. Furthermore, no distinction shall be made on the basis of the political, jurisdictional or international status of the country or territory to which a person belongs, whether it be independent, trust, non-self-governing or under any other limitation of sovereignty.

Article 3.
Everyone has the right to life, liberty and security of person.[39]

The United Nations declaration of Human Rights expressed a deep desire for freedom from so many subdued nations around the world. Countries like Indonesia (1945-1949), China (1945-1949), Cuba (1953-1959), India and Pakistan (1947), Algeria (1954-1962), Indochina (1946-1954), Vietnam (1955-1975), and all of Africa, from Ghana and Guinea to Mozambique, Zimbabwe, and finally South Africa in 1990 fought to liberate their people from colonial empires. Liberation movements within national borders also organized such as the African Americans in the Civil Rights Movement for example, or the United States indigenous peoples led by the American Indian Movement and others.

Eskimo Power in Canada

Before 1951, successive amendments to Canada's Indian Act prohibited indigenous peoples from organizing religious ceremonies and forced them to send their children to residential schools (1884). Amendments in 1914 and 1925 outlawed dancing in and off reserves, while another amendment in 1927 prohibited them from hiring a lawyer or discussing land claims. These were considered criminal offences under the Indian Act.[40] Aboriginal peoples did not have the right to vote. An "Indian" who completed post-secondary education lost his or her status as an "Indian," as did children of an indigenous woman married to a non-indigenous man.

Through the residential schools regime many indigenous people nonetheless became literate. They could read, understand the content of newspapers and start to write their own story on their own terms. The Indian-Eskimo Association of Canada, supported by the very religious organizations involved in maintaining a network of residential schools lobbied the federal government, with full support of the oil and gas industry, and facilitated the organization of national aboriginal organizations in Canada. The Indian Brotherhood and the Eskimo Brotherhood were founded in 1968. The big issue at stake for governments and corporations was to clarify ancestral land titles, if such a thing existed in law, to determine whether it could hinder access to resources, such as oil and gas in the Beaufort Sea, or hydroelectricity in northern Quebec.

As Paolo Freire argued in his book *Pedagogy of the Oppressed* published in 1970, literacy is a necessary path to political emancipation. Harold Cardinal, a member of the Sucker Creek First Nation and the youngest President of the Indian Association of Alberta opened the door to an indigenous Canadian critical political literature by publishing *The Unjust Society* in 1969, and in response to Indian Affairs Minister Jean Chrétien's White Paper, *The Red Paper*, or *Citizen Plus* in 1970. He followed up with *The Rebirth of the Canadian Indian* in 1977. A new and important narrative on the history of Canada from the point of view of indigenous peoples was emerging and venting accumulated frustration. This allowed a younger generation to be proud of their inheritance.

The same year that Jean Chrétien, the Minister of Indian Affairs and Northern Development in the Trudeau Government, launched his 'White Paper', *Statement of the Government of Canada on Indian Policy*, in 1969, proposing to do away with the Indian Act and the Indian Status in Canada, the Nisga'a of British Columbia brought their case to the Supreme Court of Canada claiming that the creation of the Province of British Columbia in 1871 had not extinguished their ancestral title to their ancestral land in the Naas valley.[41] They didn't clearly win their case, but six out of seven Supreme Court judges in Canada asserted in a 1973 judgement that there was such thing as an aboriginal title in the Canadian law. Only three judges agreed that this ancestral title was not extinguished by the creation of the province of British Colombia.[42] That recognition hailed a new era in the relationship between the Crown and the original peoples of the land. In 1973, the federal government created an Office of land claims. On November 15 of the same year, Justice Malouf ordered the complete stop of the construction of infrastructure for the Hydro-Quebec dam project of LG2, in James Bay *Eeyou* Istchee (Cree territory). The Bourassa government sat down, negotiated, and reached the James Bay and Northern Quebec Agreement that was signed in 1975 with the Eeyou Istchee Crees and the northern Quebec Inuit. It was the first comprehensive land claims agreement signed by the federal government and a provincial government and included some institutions of self-government.

For Nunavut Inuit, it took seventeen years for their organizations to negotiate the Nunavut Land Claims Agreement that was finally signed in 1993. The agreement included Article 4, the creation of a new Canadian territory, homeland of the Inuit that would be called Nunavut.[43]

Building a government infrastructure from scratch!

Three parties took part in the creation of Nunavut: the federal government, the Northwest Territories territorial government, and the political organization representing the Nunavut Inuit, the Nunavut Tunngavik Inc. (NTI). If the Nunavut Land Claims Agreement was mainly a land sharing agreement, the proposal therein of a Nunavut public government was a way to assert a form of Inuit self-government through a public government administration. Since the Inuit comprised the majority of the population in Nunavut, the Nunavut Legislative Assembly would have a majority of Inuit representatives, or Members of the Legislative Assembly. Theoretically, the new Legislative Assembly would protect Inuit language and culture and promote Inuit training and employment in the government workforce.

The second party involved was the Northwest Territories government, which already provided services to the Eastern Arctic. The division would have the consequence of depleting the capital Yellowknife of hundreds of jobs in the civil service. But at the same time, it would change the demographic balance of the territory. With the creation of Nunavut, the non-indigenous population of the Northwest Territories would become a majority, as was the case in the Yukon. Nunavut would become the exception in the Canadian federation, a jurisdiction serving a majority of an indigenous population. That, interestingly, was the unattained dream of Louis Riel!

The third party was the federal government, which had to approve and finance the whole process. In the case of a territory, the responsible federal minister has the final word on any decision taken at the territorial council or assembly, which is not the case for a province. The federal government saw in the creation of Nunavut an opportunity to assert its sovereignty over the Northwest Passage and the High Arctic Islands by confirming the traditional occupancy of the area by Canadian Inuit. Another pressing issue to sign land claims was to clarify aboriginal title and allow resource extraction companies to work within a clear legal framework.

In 1993 the three parties agreed to establish a commission to devise a plan and a timeline to set up the new territorial government. It was called the Nunavut Implementation Commission (NIC). Each partner appointed three commissioners to the NIC and John Amagoalik, a former president of Inuit Tapirisat of Canada, was selected to chair the Commission.

Since the process to create Nunavut is well documented, this text aims to stress some of the key orientations the Commission provided for the Nunavut of the future.

Decentralization

Nunavut offered the possibility to develop a government closer to the people and their daily concerns. A main recommendation of the Nunavut Implementation Commission was to create a decentralized administration that would divide government jobs among ten smaller Nunavut communities and thus avoid a concentration of civil servants in the capital who were from outside the territory. The level of decision-making devolved to these regional offices was a serious issue for the commissioners. Why not decentralize whole departments, some argued? Eventually, decentralization did not imply any devolution of power from the Legislative Assembly to the smaller communities, but a delocalization of employment.

Gender parity

Another major proposal of the Nunavut Implementation Commission was to include gender parity in the makeup of the new Legislative Assembly. Each constituency would elect one man and one woman representative to the assembly. This proposal was put to a plebiscite on May 26, 1997.[44] It was rejected 57 percent to 43 percent. Thirty-nine percent of the eligible voters cast a vote.

The gender parity proposal was a worldwide first. Only Tunisia has since passed a law, in 2016, to enforce gender parity in local councils.[45] Manitok Thompson, Minister of Community and Regional Affairs in the Government of the

Northwest Territories from 1995 to 1999 and future minister in the Nunavut cabinet, opposed the proposal with
the argument that it would discriminate against women
by not being able to compete with male candidates. Some
opposed the proposal for religious concerns, because for
some, God supposedly created men as the leaders of the
family. Obviously many Inuit men argued that the place
of a woman was in the house, taking care of children. In
ancient times, there was a clear gender division of labour,
and a skilled hunter needed a skilled seamstress in the
igloo because without appropriate clothing and footwear,
no hunter could hunt successfully.

With the transformation of the nomadic way of life
of the Inuit into a more sedentary mode in communities
developed around government services, the traditional
gender division of labour shifted dramatically. Education
became available in communities and more Inuit girls than
boys graduated. Inuit women became more employable
than men. Sixty-five percent of Nunavut government Inuit
employees are women.[46] Mostly educated as hunters, Inuit
men are more reluctant to sit and be immobilized in a classroom for hours, basically listening to a foreign instructor
presenting material mostly consigned in books published
for southern readers. More women thus became the wage
earners of the family often reversing the traditional roles
of who put food on the table. Within companies or corporations, Inuit women accessed management positions, putting them in a position of authority over their Inuit male
employees. Even if this argument was not openly debated
during the gender parity campaign, it was surely a concern
of the NIC commissioners to have elected members with
a higher level of education who would be able to decipher
bills presented to the assembly for adoption.

Electoral system

Another task of the Nunavut Implementation Commission was to decide on an electoral system. The Commission decided to import the political system of the Northwest Territories. The Northwest Territories government operated in a very straightforward manner inherited from the British parliamentary system. Each constituency elects a representative to the Legislative Assembly. These members of the assembly vote for the Premier and six cabinet members. The Premier then distributes portfolios among cabinet members. He or she can shuffle the cabinet, discipline, and remove a minister from office, but in turn the whole caucus of members can remove the Premier. The Northwest Territory Government and the Nunavut Government are still the only two jurisdictions in Canada operating on a consensus basis. A consensus government means that each member runs for election as an individual without being loyal to a political party. A decision is made when consensus among the cabinet members is reached. Then the bill is introduced to the Legislative Assembly and all members vote on it. The cabinet needs ordinary members' votes to obtain a majority at the Assembly. In 1999, the Legislative assembly had 19 members and is now at 22 members. The Yukon territorial government functions with political parties.

End of regional boards and devolution processes

Before division, the Government of the Northwest Territories made serious efforts to bring its administration closer to local communities. It authorized the creation of regional boards to make decisions in Health and Education. In each region of Nunavut, Baffin, Kivalliq (formerly

Keewatin), and Kitikmeot, elected boards managed the education budget and the health budget for the regions. A last-minute attempt was made by the department of Community and Regional Affairs and its minister Manitok Thompson to devolve more powers to hamlet councils with the Keewatin (nowadays Kivalliq) pilot project, under a policy entitled Community Empowerment. This policy would have transferred to a regional authority the region Northwest Territories government infrastructure and the annual budget to maintain it. Nunavut Tunngavik Inc. and the Nunavut Implementation Commission firmly opposed this policy, arguing that it would undercut the Nunavut government plan to have only two levels of government, territorial and municipal.[47] Since the Nunavut government was a kind of response to the Northwest Territories government administration of the Eastern Arctic, relations were often tense and controversial in the process leading to the creation of Nunavut. Hundred of jobs, assets, and money were being shuffled from West to East.

Office of the Interim Commissioner (OIC)

Once the Nunavut Interim Commission reports were published, the Minister of Indian Affairs and Northern Development, Jane Stewart, appointed Jack Anawak as the Interim Commissioner of Nunavut in April 1997. His mandate was to implement the Commission's recommendations, as stipulated in the Nunavut Act, an act allowing for the creation of Nunavut passed in parliament in 1993.[48] In order to take the job, Jack Anawak had to resign as the elected Liberal Member of Parliament for the Eastern Arctic riding of Nunatsiaq. To develop the embryo of the emerging government, DIAND established a $150 million, which was to cover the $10 million operating budget of the Office of the Interim Commissioner, the hiring of deputy ministers and senior civil servants, and the construction of minimal required infrastructures. Eleven deputy ministers were first hired. Only three of the eleven deputy ministers selected were Inuit. They had two years to prepare departments budgets, rent office space, and sub-contract government operations to the Government of the Northwest Territories, until sufficient capacity was reached in Nunavut.

The OIC was immediately faced with the challenge of finding enough competent Inuit civil servants, who had the necessary educational and professional experience for the tasks at hand in operating a government. The fourteen assistant deputy ministers afterward selected by the OIC were all Inuit. Here is what the Interim Commissioner had to say about the challenge to hire professional Inuit to work for the Government of Nunavut in November of 1998:

> Better than 50 per cent of new Nunavut government staff hired so far are Inuit, but a shortage of qualified professionals has presented an obstacle to recruitment, Interim Commissioner Jack Anawak reported this week.
>
> That means the vast majority of government positions in senior finance, legal services, engineering, health and information technology will have to be filled by non-Inuit – for the foreseeable future, at least.
>
> Speaking to delegates to Nunavut Tunngavik Inc.'s annual general meeting in Cambridge Bay on Tuesday, Anawak said more Inuit must be encouraged to enter the professions to ensure that all departments of the Nunavut government can be staffed at representative levels.[49]

From the day Anawak made that declaration in 1998 to the present day, the challenge of relying on trained Inuit professionals has been the main hurdle in the creation of Nunavut as envisioned by the land claims negotiators and a large majority of the Inuit population. Article 23 of the Nunavut Land Claims Agreement assumed that 85 percent of the Nunavut government employees should be Inuit. In reality, since the creation of the government in 1999, the Inuit employment has hovered between 45 percent and 55 percent but mostly in menial jobs such as receptionists, or maintenance staff.

A special effort was made by Nunavut Arctic College to graduate Inuit teachers in the Nunavut Teacher Education Program. Inuit women seem to go further in post-secondary education than Inuit men and consequently become much more employable.

If it has been a challenge to hire Inuit trained professional for senior positions, it also has been a challenge to hire Inuit men in relative equal numbers of women in the GN workforce.

In March of 2004, according to the GN's numbers, there were 1,079 beneficiaries working at the GN and its various agencies. Of those, 775 were Inuit women, and only 304 were Inuit men.

For non-Inuit, the ratio was more even: 683 non-Inuit men versus 789 non-Inuit women.

Recent numbers also show that the education system echoes this gender imbalance. They show that too few Inuit men, for whatever reason, are getting the scholastic qualifications that make good jobs easier to get.

High school graduation figures over the past six years show that in Nunavut, women made up 54 per cent of high school graduates. (...)

But it's at the post-secondary level that the numbers get totally off-kilter. This year, at the Nunatta campus of Arctic College, 64 women and 27 men are expected to graduate with various types of certificates and diplomas.

Nunavut Sivuniksavut, a pre-university preparation program based in Ottawa, graduated 17 women and only three men this year. Last year, they graduated 15 women and only two men.[50]

An error in the drafting?

Before division there was a perception among Dènè and Inuit that the non-indigenous minority mostly living in the capital monopolized government resources and agenda primarily for the benefit of their own business-oriented priorities. Yellowknife looked more like an average Canadian small town with sidewalks, asphalt, street lights, nice hotels and restaurants, and parks, than Iqaluit or Rankin Inlet for example, which had only gravel roads and basic services. Like Whitehorse, Yellowknife was a town with a non-indigenous majority. The western part of the territory had two operating gold mines (Con Mine and Giant Mine) in 1999, and the diamond industry was on the verge of creating thousands of jobs. In the Eastern Arctic people had the perception that the important decisions made for them were taken by far-flung bureaucrats that had virtually no down-to-earth experience with the people they served. Before division, indigenous peoples, Inuit, Métis and Dènès, formed the majority of the population of the Northwest Territories.

In 1999, at the time of the inauguration and celebrations, Inuit were enthusiastic about their new territory and this naïve and humorous conception of the new government from many could be heard all over. "Our new Inuit government will gather all of you white people working up here, put you on a big ship and send you back down South where you belong!" At least, we will be able to make our own decisions! There was a craving for a different style of administration that would be focused on Inuit specific concerns.

The Eastern Arctic, a colony of Yellowknife?

The idea of splitting the Northwest Territories first came up under the Conservative Diefenbaker government and it was pushed forward by the western part of the territory. The Eastern Arctic was then perceived as an impediment to the development of the West and the development of a responsible government as they already had in Yukon. A bill was introduced to Parliament in 1963 to proceed with division, but it died on the order paper as the Conservatives lost to the Liberals led by Lester B. Pearson Liberal in April.[51] In 1963, the Eastern Arctic was almost untouched by sustained government services. Most Inuit families were still living in hunting and fishing camps at the time, as the first government housing projects were built. In the Eastern Arctic public infrastructures had to be built from scratch.

On all aspects, the level of institutional development in the Eastern Arctic lagged behind the Mackenzie regions until division in 1999. For example, according to the Med Emerg report, in 1995, there were 167 acute beds in five hospitals in the main centres of the western regions of the Northwest Territories.[52] The same report does not give any precise figures for the Eastern Arctic for the same year, but it suggests building a new hospital in Iqaluit, and health centres in Rankin Inlet and Cambridge Bay, because the three facilities were outdated. Delivering health care in Nunavut, including staff recruitment and retention, are continuing challenges to this day. What we know, however, is that the new hospital completed in 2007 in Iqaluit has a capacity of 35 acute beds. Before division, the Baffin Regional Hospital had some 20 acute beds for all of Nunavut, when the necessary staff was available. That was 11 percent of the available acute beds of the Northwest Territories in 1995 for 39 percent of the population, the West, which represented 61 percent of the population, could count on 89 percent of the available acute beds in five regional hospitals.

In addition to these disturbing figures, the general state of health in the territory to be created was cause for concern. Indicators on infant mortality, measles, sexually transmitted diseases, mortality by lung cancer, and suicide seemed to follow a dramatic increasing curve from West to East.[53] It is understandable in such circumstances that any serious emergency case had to be medevaced by air, and any patient requiring some more sophisticated tests would have also to be flown south. In 2010, 58 percent of Nunavut patients still had to be shipped by medevac for emergencies and medical transfer. Moreover, the whole cost of medical care provided in the South to Nunavut patients consumed 40 percent of the Nunavut Department of Health budget.[54] In 1995 the rate of social assistance in the Nunavut regions was approximately three times what it was in the West.[55]

Many health problems stem from the overcrowded houses due to a severe lack of housing. In Nunavut in 2001, 13,666 people were living in 3,579 public housing households, and 98 percent of them were Inuit. When Nunavut was created, 60 percent of families living in these subsidized houses paid only $32 in rent, leaving a tab of $91 million to the Nunavut Housing Authority. In 2001, there were 4,000 people on a list to get a home from public housing.[56]

Nunavut still has practically no roads, nor does it have a deep-sea port, even though serious discussions about the development of one have been conducted for the last twenty years by politicians of all stripes. The most recent plan proposes to have the construction of a deep-sea port in Iqaluit completed by the fall of 2020.[57] Means of transportation are mainly by air, sea, or over the snow and ice in winter by snowmobile. These are all costly and at the mercy of fluctuating fuel prices. Since all electricity comes from diesel-powered generators, fuel prices directly impact electricity rates.

As mentioned above, a huge challenge to the new government is still to find in Nunavut the required technical skills to run a government. At the time of division, more than 50 percent of Nunavut adults didn't have a secondary diploma.[58] Article 23 of the Nunavut Land Claims Agreement states that the Nunavut government workforce should have 85 percent of Inuit employment, to reflect the ethnic component of the territory. Between 1993 and 2000, the federal government injected $39.9 million to train Inuit for civil service jobs in a program called Nunavut Unified Human Resources Development Strategy, NUHRDS. But the federal funding for training dried up after 2000. In 2006, Nunavut Tunngavik Inc. filed a lawsuit for one billion dollars against Ottawa for not providing funding for Inuit training and thus not implementing the Nunavut Land Claims Agreement.

Sixteen years after division, the federal government finally acknowledged the fact that it did not fulfill its obligation to provide training for Inuit in order to reach a similar proportion of Government of Nunavut employees as in the population. For 16 years in the formative years of the new territory, Nunavut Inuit didn't benefit from the level of training as stipulated in the Agreement. In 2015, the Conservative federal government settled the case with Nunavut Tunngavik Inc. for $255 million.[59]

All these factors have certainly not facilitated the task of the emerging government!

Cheap change!

In light of the dire situation of the Nunavut regions, one would expect that creating a new jurisdiction would require extraordinary means. One wonders if this was the approach chosen by both levels of governments.

1) Minimal funding for creating a territory from scratch

After months of suspense, in May 1996, the Minister of Indian Affairs and Northern Development, Ron Irwin, finally announced a budget of $149.9 million to be spent between 1996 and 2000 to set up the new government. Parties involved in the division process besides the federal senior bureaucrats were at first in shock. The late John Ningark who was the chairman of the NWTG Nunavut Caucus had this comment:

> Every member of the (NWT) Nunavut caucus that I talked to were very disappointed about the mere $150 million that would be used for the implementation of Nunavut. (...) We were under the impression, as the premier has stated that the money would be in the neighborhood of $600 million that was announced back in 1991.[60]

In June 1998, the federal government made public its decision to fund the new Nunavut government annually with $626 million. The Nunavut population was then approximately 27,000, which meant $23,185 per resident.

The western side of the Northwest Territories would also have to adapt to a new smaller government and would receive $701 million. With its population of 43,000, it would have $16,300 per person.[61]

Since fiscal revenues accounted for 30 percent of its total budget, the new budget of the Government of the Northwest Territories would dispose of approximately $1 billion to operate during the 1999 fiscal year, which meant $23,286 per person. The Nunavut Government, however, could not count on any significant economic activity which meant fiscal revenue would be minimal, between 0 and 5 percent.

The two new territories would then operate on a very similar per capita basis. Bernadette Makpah, Nunavut Tunngavik's secretary treasurer, criticized the agreement for not taking into account the important issues of the Nunavut Inuit. Ottawa should have put much more money on the table: "Some of these would include the cost of using Inuktitut as a working language, the need for additional housing funds, and to improve socio-economic conditions in relation to the rest of Canada."[62]

Six months into the administration of the new government, Jim Bell, the astute editor of the main Nunavut paper, *Nunatsiaq News,* came to a brutal realisation:

> The Nunavut government has begun its life with a parsimonious bare-bones budget that was shaped mostly by Ottawa's Office of the Interim Commissioner. So far, it's Nunavut's inadequate budget, not the ideas and dreams of Nunavut residents and government officials that is the greatest single factor driving the formation of policy within Nunavut's fledgling government. That is not power — that is the very essence of powerlessness.[63]

The reaction from Nunavut and Northwest Territories politicians to this stingy budget was that Nunavut would have to cope with it and do the best in the circumstances. For example, one dire consequence of this lack of federal funding was the absence of a budget for a sustainable Nunavut language policy. In a report on the state of Inuktut in Nunavut released in 2017, Ian Martin, a professor of linguistics at Glendon College, York University, in Toronto, recalls that the language issue was brushed away from Nunavut budgeting discussions by senior officers of the federal Finance Department in 1998 and that these language issues should be "addressed at a later day."[64] The federal government never seriously addressed the issue.

Wasn't the main goal of Inuit leaders negotiating a public government included in the Nunavut Land Claims Agreement the protection and enhancement of Inuit culture and language?

Paul Quassa, who signed the Nunavut Land Claims Agreement for the Tunngavik Federation of Nunavut in 1993 and who was elected Premier of Nunavut in 2017, made clear in a 2003 statement that the protection of the language was at the core of Inuit concerns: "That's the whole reason why the land claims took place, because we were losing our language. I think that's part of the whole land claims process. Once you have the languages the culture is strong."[65]

Between 1996 and 2011, the use of Inuktut in Inuit homes dropped from 76 percent to 61 percent.[66]

2) Overcrowded homes

At the end of the 1980s, the Canada Mortgage and Housing Corporation stopped financing public housing projects all across Canada and also decided to withdraw completely from funding the operation and maintenance of the existing stock of public housing by planning to reduce its contribution to nothing from 1997 to 2037. The Royal Commission on Aboriginal Peoples noted the devastating impact that measure had on indigenous communities:

> Housing policy is a tough challenge, so daunting that it has been under review by the federal government since 1988 with no sign of resolution. But the situation has not been static over the past eight years: needs have been increasing, and governments have been withdrawing progressively from the field. The impasse must be broken; otherwise, the demoralizing and debilitating effects of the housing crisis could undermine efforts to improve relations between Aboriginal people and the rest of Canadian society and impede the move to greater self-reliance in other areas.[67]

Overcrowded houses are the cause of so may other problems, such as domestic violence, the spread of infectious and sexually transmitted diseases, educational problems due to lack of space for studying and homework, lung cancer caused by secondary smoke, suicide... The Nunavut Housing Corporation made the following analysis in 2001:

> The waiting list in October 1999 shows that about 1,500 families in Nunavut are waiting for some form of housing assistance. As a percentage of the population this far exceeds the National rate of 12 percent. The total withdrawal of federal funding for new social housing has put a severe strain on the government's ability to meet the housing needs of our residents.
>
> Inadequate and overcrowded housing contributes to social and health problems, such as major diseases, marriage breakdown, alcoholism and child and spousal abuse.

The financial results can be measured in terms of higher costs of health care, income support payments, policing and penitentiary service. Solving the housing problems of Northerners could reduce the cost of health services and social assistance by improving social and health standards. As long as housing problems exist for Northerners, communities will not be able to achieve wellness.[68]

3) Policies of budget austerity

In 1995, the Government of the Northwest Territories passed a law making illegal any operating deficit, the *Deficit Elimination Act*. The Premier at the time Don Morin and his Minister of Finance, John Todd, explained that they had to face a deficit of $100 million mainly caused by the increasing needs in services of the growing population of the Northwest Territories, on one hand, but also by the drastic budget cuts coming from Ottawa through their Territorial Financing Formula.[69] This was happening all across Canada under the Liberal Government and Finance Minister Paul Martin's drastic balancing of the federal budget.

These cuts targeted employees' wages and benefits, but also jobs and programs. The Northwest Territories announced clearly that it would reduce services in the coming years, arguing that the deficit needed to be eliminated before the Territories would be divided. That deficit elimination strategy then decreased the already poor level of services for the Nunavut region. The Government also decided on an infrastructure devolution strategy to the communities, which could mean at the same time dumping part of the deficit in the backyard of municipalities, including those of the Nunavut region.

4) Ottawa will not invest money in construction of infrastructure

As the federal Liberal Government aimed to eliminate its own deficit, it opted to have a private partner constructing the required infrastructures for the new Nunavut government who would then lease the facilities to the new Government of Nunavut. The private investor was the Nunavut Construction Company (NCC), owned by the corporate arms of the Nunavut regional Inuit organizations and Nunasi Corporation, the corporate arm of Nunavut Tunngavik Inc. Within four years, NCC built 12 office buildings and 250 residential housing units.

Reviewing the transactions contracted by the new government, Sheila Fraser, Canada's Auditor General, noted that as of March 2000 the Government of Nunavut had signed for $476 million in lease payments over a period of 20 years. In one of these transactions, Fraser found that the Government had paid 50 percent more than if it had bought the buildings.[70] She observed that the Government of Nunavut at the time of the signing didn't have the financial expertise to analyse their best options.

Meanwhile, the largest private company benefiting from those leases announced record benefits.[71]

5) The Government of the Northwest Territories had been selling staff housing in Nunavut just a few years before division, jeopardizing the capacity of the new government to accommodate staff.

With the rationale of eliminating the deficit before division, the Northwest Territories government got rid of its staff housing in the Eastern Arctic in the years preceding division. They sold some properties to their own staff, but the bulk of it was purchased by large real estate companies that quickly turned around to lease these facilities to the new government on 40-year leases and at stratospheric cost.[72] Jim Bell of *Nunatsiaq News* observed in 1997:

> That's because, in a lengthy section that raises many concerns with the decentralization model proposed by the NIC, the GNWT suggests that decentralization may not now be affordable.
>
> That's a legitimate concern. But coming from the GNWT, it reeks of hypocrisy. The GNWT's own policies have also made decentralization more difficult to achieve. Because of GNWT policies such as departmental amalgamation, restructuring, privatization, job layoffs, and other changes, there are fewer jobs and functions left to decentralize in Nunavut.
>
> Later on, the GNWT notes that the NTI-Ottawa infrastructure agreement, under which the construction of Nunavut's legislative assembly and other buildings will be financed by private capital, provides for supply of staff housing to some Nunavut government employees.
>
> This "has the potential to create divisiveness between employees," the GNWT says. This is the government that has been throwing employees out of staff housing for the past four years.
>
> And it's the same government that for the past two years has ignored NIC recommendations to suspend the sale of staff housing—partly because of fears that the policy will make it impossible for Nunavut to recruit new staff.[73]

6) Increase in airfare and freight rates for airline companies following NAV Canada increase in service fees[74]

The budget of the Government of Nunavut or any local organization is directly impacted by any fluctuation of airlines fees, as it is the main means of transportation between communities and southern Canada. This problem is amplified in a decentralized government, where ten government offices are spread out on an immense territory. In November 1998, Nav Canada announced a substantial hike in freight rates that substantially impacted government and corporate operations, as well as families.[75]

Conclusion

The enumeration of stumbling blocks on the road to Nunavut could go on and on. It is hoped readers will have a good idea of the enormous challenge that the new government faced from its inception on April 1, 1999. It faced 132 years of institutional negligence. Inuit leaders knew the dire conditions of existence of Inuit families in the new territory. The Inuit response to the situation is encapsulated in the title of the book, an expression dear to Paul Okalik, *Let's Move On*! Whatever adverse conditions life brings to your journey, it is of no use cultivating anger and remorse. Let's do the best with the inherited situation. That is the simple ancestral teaching that guided Paul Okalik through his years in politics. What can we do practically to improve the living conditions of Nunavut Inuit? Okalik uses the expression "That is very unfortunate" to comment on situations over which he has no control. He also uses the expression "I grew up in a tougher neighbourhood" to qualify his resilience in adversarial situations. "But let's move on" for the task at hand is huge in order to attain some broad goals envisioned by the members of the Legislative Assembly in 1999: a self-reliant healthy society, at par with the rest of Canada, and thriving in its own culture and language.[1]

Timeline

1964, May 26	Paul Okalik was born from father Auyaluk and mother Annie Okalik.
1979	Robertson High school in Frobisher Bay.
1985	Okalik began working for the Tunngavik Federation of Nunavut as a researcher and became a Deputy Chief Negotiator and the Special Assistant to the President.
1993	Signing of the Nunavut Land Claims Agreement.
1994	B.A. in Political Science and Canadian Studies from Carleton University.
1997	Law degree from the University of Ottawa.
1999	Northwest Territories Bar.
1999	Articling at Ann Crawford's legal office.
1999, February 15	Elected to the Nunavut Legislative Assembly, Iqaluit West.
1999, March 5	Okalik is voted Premier of Nunavut.
2004	Okalik is re-elected in Iqaluit West.
2004, March 5	Okalik is voted Premier of Nunavut against Tagaq Curley.

2005	Carleton University awarded Okalik an honorary Doctor of Law.
2008	Okalik re-elected in Iqaluit West.
2008, November 14	Okalik defeated by Eva Aariak as the Premier of Nunavut.
2010, November 4	Speaker of the Legislative Assembly.
2011, April 6	Okalik's resignation from the Nunavut Legislative Assembly.
2011	Okalik runs for the Liberal Party of Canada in Nunatsiaq in the Federal Election, but Conservative Leona Aglukaq wins.
2013, October 28	Okalik is elected as the MLA of Iqaluit Sinaa.
2016, March 3	Okalik resigned as a cabinet minister.
2017, October 30	Okalik lost his seat as the Member of the Nunavut Legislative Assembly for Iqaluit-Sinaa.

Notes

Inuit First

1. After the signing of the Nunavut Land Claims Agreement in 1993, the Tunngavik Federation of Nunavut changed name to Nunavut Tunngavik Inc.

2. The Nanisivik zinc-lead mine operated from 1976 to 2002. It was located near the Inuit community of Arctic Bay, in northern Baffin Island.

CHAPTER ONE. **I Was Young, Foolish, and Full of Energy!**

1. Angmarlik was the last Inuit leader at the Kekerten whaling station in the Cumberland Sound. He converted to Christianity in 1902. In 1915, Angmarlik moved to Idlungajung with many of his relatives. Angmarlik and his wife Asivak had only one child of their own, Qatsuk, the grandmother of Paul Okalik. For many years in the summertime, Angmarlik would manage the beluga whale hunt in the Cumberland Sound for the Hudson's Bay Company. Angmarlik passed away in Pangnirtung in the 1950s. The visitor Centre in Pangnirtung is named after him. See: Edward Maurice, *The Last Gentleman Adventurer: Coming of Age in the Arctic,* 166

2. Siina is more commonly known as Sedna in English. She is an Inuit legendary character who lives at the bottom of the sea and rules over the sea mammals. Hunters have to pay her respect in order to make a successful hunt.

3. Nettilling Lake is the largest lake located on an island in Canada. It is 123 kilometres long, some 300 kilometres northwest of Iqaluit.

4. Pete Mahovlich (1946-) played for different clubs of the National Hockey League. He was a Montreal Canadien player when they won

four Stanley Cups in 1971, 1973, 1976, and 1977. He was the brother of Frank Mahovlich who also played for the Montreal Canadiens with Pete and who became a member of the Canadian Senate.

5. Mike Gardener lived for more than fifty years in Nunavut. Fluent in Inuktitut, he was an Anglican Minister. He was awarded the Order of Canada in 2007 and the Order of Nunavut in 2011. Now retired, Mike Gardener resides in Iqaluit with his wife Margaret.

6. Mary Ellen Thomas worked most of her adult life as an adult educator in Nunavut. She is now the Executive Director of the Nunavut Research Institute in Iqaluit.

7. The Young Offenders Act regulating the criminal prosecution of young Canadians was passed in Parliament in 1984. In 2003, it was replaced by the Youth Criminal Justice Act. In 1988, it was consolidated into the Northwest Territories Revised Statutes.

8. Nanisivik Mine started its operation in 1975 near the small hamlet of Arctic Bay and extracted zinc and lead from the ground until 2002. At the peak of its operation, some 20 percent of its workforce of approximately two hundred miners was Inuit. Breakwater Resources was the owner of the Nanisivik Mine.

CHAPTER 2. **I Was Thinking About Tomorrow**

1. AWOL: Absent Without Official Leave.

2. Now the Qikiqtani Inuit Association.

3. Now Iqaluit.

4. David Bennett is an Ontario lawyer who served as a counsel to the Tunngavik Federation of Nunavut (Now Nunavut Tunngavik Inc.) from 1985 to 1987. He is currently Adjudicator for the Independent Assessment Process, determining whether Claimants are entitled to compensation for abuse suffered in Indian Residential Schools. See: http://www.tas-cas.org/uploads/tx_tascas/CV_Bennett_Jan2017.pdf

5. Sol Simon Reisman, OC (June 19, 1919 – March 9, 2008) was the chief negotiator of the Canada-United States Free Trade Agreement signed in 1988. It became the North American Free Trade Agreement (NAFTA) when Mexico joined the agreement in 1994. Reisman was also instrumental in the making of the Canada-U.S. Auto Pact signed in 1965.

6. The James Bay and Northern Quebec Agreement (JBNQA) was signed on November 11, 1975 between the Northern Quebec Inuit Association (NQIA), the Grand Council of the Crees, Government of Quebec, la Société d'énergie de la Baie James, la Société de développe-

ment de la Baie James, la Commission hydro-électrique de Québec, and the Government of Canada. After the signing, the NQIA transformed into the Makivik Corporation which became the Inuit body monitoring the implementation of the agreement and the management of the compensation money of $91,184,322. The Naskapi of Schefferville joined the JBNQA in 1978.

7. Charlie Watt was the founding President of the Northern Quebec Inuit Association (1972-78), and of Makivik Corporation (1978-82). Born in Kuujjuaq in 1944, Charlie Watt was appointed to the Canadian Senate in 1984 by the late former Prime Minister Pierre Elliott Trudeau. He was re-elected President of Makivik Corporation on January 18, 2018. See: http://www.parl.gc.ca/SenatorsBio/senator_biography.aspx?senator_id=103&language=E

8. The Committee for the Original People's Entitlement (*COPE*) representing the Inuvialuit (Inuit of the Western Arctic) signed the Inuvialuit Final Agreement on June 5, 1984.

CHAPTER 3. **My Studies Made Me a Proud Inuk**

1. David Paciocco was appointed a judge on the Ontario court of Justice in 2011. In 2017, he was appointed to the Ontario Court of Appeal.

2. Ottawa wanted the Duplessis government in Quebec to reimburse relief provided to Inuit experiencing dire situations in northern Quebec. The Quebec government refused and took the federal government to the superior court, which judged in favour of Quebec, asserting that indigenous peoples were a federal responsibility. See: Bonesteel, Sarah, *Canada's Relationship with Inuit: A History of Policy and Program Development*. 2006. Indigenous and Northern Affairs Canada.P. 25. http://www.aadnc-aandc.gc.ca/eng/1100100016900/1100100016908#chp2

CHAPTER 4. **We Had to Make the Government Work**

1. David Paciocco is now a judge at the Ontario Court of Justice. From 1982 he was a common law professor at the University of Ottawa. In 2005 David Paciocco received an honorary doctorate from the Laurentian University.

2. Cup-a-Soup is a soup sold in powder by Lipton product that has to be mixed with boiling water.

3. The Nunavut Teacher Education Program (NTEP) is a post-secondary program delivered by Nunavut Arctic College. It was originally delivering a Certificate in Native & Northern Education from McGill

University in two years. From 1994, with an additional academic year students could obtain a Baccalaureate in Education. In 2007, NTEP made a new partnership with the University of Regina to monitor the program. Many NTEP students pursue their post-secondary studies to obtain a Masters degree in Education, delivered by the Prince Edward Island University. Since 1999, the NTEP program has been delivered in different Nunavut communities.

4. Akitsiraq law school was a legal study program provided in Iqaluit by Victoria University in partnership with Nunavut Arctic College. Eleven students graduated in 2005. There was an attempt to repeat the experience in 2011 in partnership with the University of Ottawa, but the Government of Nunavut didn't provide the funding. The Minister of Education announced the re-opening of the program in 2016. Since fall 2017, the Akitsiraq law school has been in full operation at the Nunavut Arctic College in Iqaluit in partnership with the University of Saskatchewan starting in the Fall of 2017.

5. Ann Crawford is a long time practicing lawyer in Iqaluit, Nunavut. She opened her law practice in 1986. She was later involved in many Government of Nunavut initiatives. She was the Nunavut cabinet secretary, CEO of the Qulliq energy corporation, and was also involved in creation of the Akitsiraq Law School Society.

6. Flash Kilabuk was an Iqaluit city councillor at different occasions and mayor from 1997 to 2000. He passed away in April 2013.

7. In June 2003, the late James Arvaluk had to resign as Minister of Education and Member of the Legislative Assembly after being convicted of assault causing bodily harm. He was representing the riding of Tunnuniq. James Arvaluk passed away in April 2016.

8. Following the 1992 plebiscite on the division of the Northwest Territories and the signing of the Nunavut Land Claims Agreement in 1993, the Nunavut Implementation Commission was created in 1994 to advise the federal government, the Government of the Northwest Territories, and Nunavut Tunngavik Inc. on the plans to create the Government of Nunavut. The Commission produced two reports: Footsteps in New Snow I and II. In 1997, the then Minister of Indian Affairs (now Aboriginal Affairs) and Northern Development, Ron Irwin, created the Office of the Interim Commissioner to put in place an embryo of the future Government of Nunavut and its departments, following the NIC planning. Jack Anawak was appointed Interim Commissioner.

9. Peter Kilabuk became Minister of Education in November 2000 and organized a large consultation of Nunavut communities to pro-

pose a new draft for an Education Act. On March 2003, the Standing Committee on Health and Education rejected the proposed education bill mainly on a language issue, that the bill was too much English speaking oriented and didn't support enough Inuktitut and French education. A month later, Premier Okalik shuffled the cabinet and Peter Kilabuk was moved from Education to the Department of Culture, Language, Elders and Youth (CLEY).

10. The decentralization of the Nunavut Government was a recommendation of the Nunavut Implementation Commission to prevent the capital Iqaluit to become a huge administrative centre, out of touch with smaller remote communities, similarly to what happened in the Northwest Territories with its capital Yellowknife. Including the capital, eleven communities were selected to receive government positions. The decentralization process was never intended to share decision making with smaller communities but only to spread government jobs more evenly throughout the territory.

11. See: http://www.nunatsiaqonline.ca/archives/nunavut990730/nvt90709_01.html

12. See: http://www.nunatsiaqonline.ca/archives/nunavut990625/nvt90625_01.html

13. Jim Bell, "Time Zone Debate a Waste of Energy." *Nunatsiaq News*, October 1, 1999: http://www.nunatsiaqonline.ca/archives/nunavut991030/editorial.html

14. Jack Anawak publicly opposed a decision of the cabinet to move thirteen positions of the petroleum products division from Rankin Inlet to Baker Lake, which was contrary to the principle of solidarity and secrecy of the cabinet that had taken that decision. Jack Anawak was stripped of his Culture, Language, Elders and Youth portfolio by Premier Okalik in March 2003. http://www.nunatsiaqonline.ca/archives/nunavut030214/news/nunavut/30214_01.html

CHAPTER 5. **My Role Was to Lead and Make Things Work**

1. For the text of the Bathurst Mandate see: http://socrates.acadiau.ca/courses/pols/inspired/content/pdf/Pinasuaqtavut_Healthy_Communities.pdf

2. Simon Tookoomee (1934-2010) was born and raised in the Back River area. Threatened by starvation, his family moved to Baker Lake in the 1960s. Simon Tookoomee became a renowned Baker Lake artist who was also involved in the development of the Sanavik Cooperative.

3. Nunavummi Nangminiqaqtunik Ikajuuti, the NNI policy (http://nni. gov.nu.ca/policy) was developed by Nunavut Tunngavik Incorporated and the Government of Nunavut to favour Nunavut businesses and Inuit owned businesses in the attribution of government contracts in accordance with section 24 of the Nunavut Land Claims Agreement (http://nlca.tunngavik.com/).

4. Institut national des langues et civilisations orientales is part of Université de la Sorbonne in Paris. http://www.inalco.fr/institut/universite-sorbonne-paris-cite

5. The *Nunavut Human Rights Act* was passed by the Nunavut Legislative Assembly on November 5, 2003. http://nhrt.ca/english/home

CHAPTER 6. **You Have to Be Decisive, and Act Quickly**

1. Direct appointments do not have to go through the process of competition to hire staff.

2. Cumberland Resources Ltd. has conducted exploration some 70 kilometres north of Baker Lake since 1995. In 2002 the company announced that the amount of gold found was then sufficient to start the extraction of the Meadowbank gold deposit. Agnico-Eagle purchased the Meadowbank gold project from Cumberland Resources in 2007 and produced its first gold bar in 2010. Agnico Eagle is now considering developing another gold mine site at the Meliadine deposit located some 24 kilometres north of Rankin Inlet.

3. In February 2003, Premier Paul Okalik stripped minister Jack Anawak of his portfolio of the Department of Culture, Language, Elders and Youth after Anawak had publicly criticized the government for moving thirteen positions from Rankin Inlet to Baker Lake. Jack Anawak was also removed from the cabinet by a vote of the ordinary members of the Legislative Assembly. http://www.nunatsiaqonline. ca/archives/nunavut030307/news/nunavut/30307_02.html

4. David Simailak was asked to resign from the Nunavut cabinet on Dec. 11, 2007 by Premier Paul Okalik after it was demonstrated that he had frequent information exchanges with his personal business trustee even from his ministerial office and computer. http://www.nunatsiaqonline.ca/archives/2008/809/80919/news/nunavut/80919_1533.html

CHAPTER 7. **It's Still Taking Us Too Long to Catch Up**

1. "Standing Committees fulfill three important functions: the study of legislation, the examination of policy issues and the review of gov-

ernment spending proposals." From: http://www.assembly.nu.ca/
standing-and-special-committees

2. *The Nunavut Official Languages Act* was approved on June 4,
2008 by the Nunavut Legislative Assembly, replacing the previous
Northwest Territory Languages Act that was stressing the importance
of nine aboriginal languages without conferring them equal status to
French and English. The new Nunavut Official Languages Act gives
to the Inuit language (Inuktut) equal status to French and English in
Nunavut. *The Nunavut Official Languages Act* was approved by the
Parliament of Canada, on June 11, 2009.

3. The term Inuktut is generally accepted to designate all different
forms of the Inuit language in the Arctic.

4. Inuinaqtun is the form of Inuit language spoken in the western
region of Nunavut.

5. The Knud Rasmussen Folk High School in Sisimiut, Greenland
was created in 1962 with the mission of developing programs enhan-
cing Inuit culture and language. The Nunavut Piqqusilirivvik cultural school, a division of Nunavut Arctic College, was created by
the Government of Nunavut following an official visit to Greenland
by officials from the Government and Nunavut Tunngavik Inc. The
Piqqusilirivvik cultural school building was completed in 2010 in
the community of Clyde River. http://www.nunatsiaqonline.ca/
archives/50211/news/nunavut/50211_02.html

6. Louis Tapardjuk has been an advocate of Inuit culture and language
all his life; first with the Arctic Co-operatives movement, and later with
the Igloolik Oral History project. He was elected as the MLA for the
Amtituq riding from 2004 to 2013. He was voted in the cabinet where
he held the portfolios of the Departments of Culture, Language, Elders
and Youth, and of Finance.

7. *Nunavut Official Languages Act*, and the *Inuit Language Protection
Act*. *The Nunavut Official Languages Act* was approved by the
Nunavut Legislative Assembly in 2008 and came into force on April
1, 2013.

8. In November 2002, Nunavut Premier Paul Okalik introduced the
first human rights bill. In 2005, he was officially supporting same sex
marriage in Canada. These issues are very controversial in Nunavut
and in 2014, Paul Okalik took a clear public stance in support of the gay
and lesbian Nunavut community. On all these occasions, Paul Okalik
was seriously criticized publicly and privately.

CHAPTER 8. **I Don't Just Sit There and Smile and Clap My Hands**
1. Only four previous Members of the Nunavut Legislative Assembly out of nineteen were re-elected in the 2008 territorial election: Tagaq Curley, Paul Okalik, Louis Tapardjuk, and Hunter Tootoo. Eva Aariak was selected as the new Premier.
2. In May of 2009, Eva Aariak appointed former Yukon premier Piers McDonald to conduct a complete review of the operations of the Government of Nunavut. McDonald handed in the Qanukkanniq report card on October 1, 2009 basically stating how the expectations of the people for Nunavut had not been met since the creation of the new territory. See: http://www.nunatsiaqonline.ca/stories/article/961_blunt_report_recommends_sweeping_changes_to_gn/
3. The Order of Nunavut was created by the Nunavut Legislative Assembly in December 2009. An advisory council comprising the speaker of the Legislative Assembly, the senior judge of the Nunavut Court of Justice, and the president of Nunavut Tunngavik Inc. recommends the candidates to be honoured by the award.
4. The Kelowna Accord was an agreement between the federal, provincial, and territorial governments and Canadian aboriginal organizations on a five-year plan to improve the living conditions of Canadian First Nations, Métis, and Inuit. The Accord emerged from eighteen months of consultation by the Paul Martin Liberal Government and planned five billion dollars over five years to implement the Accord. In 2006, the newly elected Conservative minority government of Stephen Harper didn't follow suit.
5. In Yukon, the Conservative candidate Ryan Leef was elected at the 2011 election, replacing the Liberal Larry Bagnell who had represented the riding for more than ten years (2000-2011) after winning four federal elections.
6. The federal riding of Nunavut covers all of the Nunavut Territory. Before 1997, it used to be called Nunatsiaq, then the eastern part of the Northwest Territories.
7. Nunavut Land Claims Agreement: 5.7.26 – Licensing: Subject to the terms of this Article, an Inuk with proper identification may harvest up to his or her adjusted basic needs level without any form of licence or permit and without imposition of any form of tax or fee.
8. Louis Tapardjuk was forced to resign in January 2009 as a cabinet minister after the content of a letter he wrote stating that men were not always the ones to blame in domestic disputes was made public.

He was the only minister to serve under both the Okalik government and the Aariak government.

CHAPTER 9. Southern Canada Did Not Get Developed Without National Support

1. Gary Albert Doer was the Premier of Manitoba from 1999 to 2009, as the leader of a New Democratic Party government. Prime Minister Stephen Harper appointed Gary Doer as the Canadian Ambassador to the United States in 2009.

2. The First Ministers' Meeting on health care presided by Prime Minister Jean Chrétien was held in Ottawa on February 4-5, 2003.

3. Ernie Larry Eves became Premier of Ontario in 2002, replacing the previous conservative Premier Mike Harris. In 2003, his government was defeated by the Liberals of Dalton McGuinty. In Quebec, the Parti Québécois government was elected in 1998. Bernard Landry was appointed Premier in 2001 but was defeated by the Liberals and Jean Charest in 2003. Bernard Landry resigned as the party leader in 2005.

4. A road linking Rankin Inlet in the Kivalliq region of Nunavut to the Manitoba road network would cover 1,100 kilometres in a very difficult terrain and would cost some 1.2 billion dollars according to a 2010 feasibility study. See: http://www.gov.nu.ca/sites/default/files/Nunavut_Manitoba_Business_Case_executive_summary.pdf

5. In May 2003 the Canadian Food Inspection Agency found a case of mad cow disease, bovine spongiform encephalopathy, in Northern Alberta. The United States immediately closed its border, as well as forty other countries, to the import of Canadian cattle meat.

6. The Kelowna Accord was concluded in November of 2005, in the town of Kelowna B.C., between the federal Liberal government of Paul Martin, the provinces, territories, and main aboriginal organizations aiming at improving the livelihood of aboriginal Canadians mainly in the areas of health, education, housing, and relationships to the federal government. http://www.international.alberta.ca/documents/Canadian_Intergovernmental_Relations/800044004_e.pdf?0.970948780188337

7. Paul Martin's government was defeated in the January 2006 federal election. The Stephen Harper's Conservative party won 124 seats against 103 for the Liberal Party, 51 for the Bloc québécois, and 29 for the NDP.

8. There were only two First Ministers' Meetings held under the Stephen Harper Conservative government: the first one in November 2008, and the second one in January 2009.

9. The territorial council is formed by the selected ministers and is also designated in the territories by the most usual term, cabinet.

10. *The Home Rule Act* was passed in 1979 by the Parliament of the Kingdom of Denmark, ceding many political responsibilities to a Greenland elected assembly, Kalaallit Nunaanni Inatsisartut, the Greenland Parliament. Foreign affairs, defence, criminal courts, subsurface rights remained within Copenhagen jurisdiction.

11. The Nanisivik mine operated from 1976 to 2002, extracting zinc and lead, near the hamlet of Arctic Bay on Baffin Island.

12. Nunavummi Nangminiqaqtunik Ikajuuti or NNI was implemented in April 2000 by the Government of Nunavut to give a competitive advantage to Inuit businesses and to a lesser degree to Nunavut businesses bidding on public contracts.

13. In December 2006, NTI filed a court case against the Government of Canada for not fulfilling its obligation stipulated in Article 23 of the Nunavut Land Claims Agreement for adequately training an Inuit workforce and increasing the percentage of Inuit employment in the Government of Nunavut to the proportion of Inuit in the Nunavut population. The court case was settled by the parties involved outside the court in May 2015. http://www.nunatsiaqonline.ca/stories/article/65674ottawa_settles_with_nunavut_inuit_pays_255.5m_in_compensation/

CHAPTER 10. **We Used to Deal with Problems Right Away, and Move On**
1. Canada: *Corrections and Conditional Release Act*, S.C. 1992, c. 20. http://laws-lois.justice.gc.ca/eng/acts/c-44.6/page-1.html

CHAPTER 11. **Still Frozen in Time!**
1. The major decision taken by the Government of Nunavut under Eva Aariak premiership (2011-2013) was the upgrading of the Iqaluit airport through a Public Private Partnership (PPP) at a total cost of $418.9 million to be paid over 30 years. The construction started in July 2014. The airport was officially opened on August 9, 2017. Fifteen percent of the labour force during construction should be Inuit.

2. http://www.nunatsiaqonline.ca/stories/article/65674nunavut_officials_promise_inuit_training_on_iqaluit_airport_scheme/

3. Paul Okalik is referring to a famous statement made by Jose Kusugak in 2004, who was then the President of Inuit Tapiriit Kanatami: "In accepting Canada, we shouldn't have to worry about losing our identity

or believing in ourselves any less. Inuit are more than First Canadians, Inuit are Canadians first." https://www.itk.ca/media/media-release/first-canadians-canadians-first

4. The new icebreaker construction plan was delayed by the Conservative government and the Canadian Coast Guard will still use the old icebreakers until 2021-2022. http://www.cbc.ca/news/politics/arctic-icebreaker-delayed-as-tories-prioritize-supply-ships-1.1991522

5. In 2012, Prime Minister Stephen Harper announced the creation of the Canadian High Arctic Research Station (CHARS) to be built in the hamlet of Cambridge Bay (1,600 inhabitants) at a cost of $142 million. The facility opened its doors in 2017.

CHAPTER 12. **Doing My Part to Contribute to Nunavut**
1. The Nunavut Legislature has now 22 Members.
2. Stephen Kafkwi was elected at the Legislative Assembly of the Northwest Territories in 1987 for the Sahtu constituency. He was Premier from 2000 to 2003. Prior to that, Kafkwi was elected as the President of the Dènè nation.
3. Dennis Fentie was the Yukon Premier for the Conservative Yukon party from 2002 to 2011.

Im Out!
1. In December 2014, a video clip of Leona Aglukkaq reading a newspaper during a House of Commons question period on the price of food in the North went viral. http://www.cbc.ca/news/politics/leona-aglukkaq-admits-reading-newspaper-was-a-bad-idea-during-question-period-1.2859631
2. McCArthy, Shawn and Jeff Lewis. "Washington to ban offshore oil and gas licenses in Arctic waters." *The Globe and Mail*, December 10, 2016. http://www.theglobeandmail.com/news/politics/ottawa-to-ban-offshore-oil-and-gas-licences-in-arctic-waters/article33392589/
3. The Department of Indigenous and Northern Affairs was split in two by the Trudeau government in August 2017: the Department of Crown-Indigenous Relations and Northern Affairs, and the Department of Indigenous Services.
4. See *Nuantsiaq Online,* 22 January 2016.

Nunavut: The Long Road Before – Historical Context

1. Maurice Bulbulian's *Dancing Around the Table,* a National Film Board production, is a great introduction to this complex subject. https://www.nfb.ca/film/dancing_around_the_table_1/. Two of these conferences were held under the Pierre Elliott Trudeau Liberal Government (1983-1984), and the two last ones were held under the Brian Mulroney Conservative Government (1985-1987). Trudeau resigned from office a week before the 1984 conference. It was directly against his convictions to allow a special status to any Canadian minority, as he was dead against any '*statut particulier*', or asymmetrical federalism for the Province of Quebec.

2. L'Abbé, Francis, "Le litige territorial à l'origine de la crise d'Oka n'est toujours pas réglé." Radio-Canada, July 10, 2015.

3. RCAP, A Word from Commissioners. 1996 http://www.aadnc-aandc.gc.ca/eng/1100100014597/1100100014637

4. *Paul Aarulaaq Quassa. We Need to Know Who We Are.* Edited By Louis McComber. Iqaluit, 2008. Nunavut Arctic College. P. 97. *We helped to improve the image of the Conservative government then.*

5. Thomas Berger, Conciliator's Final Report, The Nunavut Project: 2006. P. 13.

6. Thomas Berger, Conciliator's Final Report, The Nunavut Project: 2006. P. 13.

7. Innis, Harold. (1930-1977) *The Fur Trade in Canada: An Introduction to Canadian Economic History.* Revised and reprinted. Toronto: University of Toronto Press, p. 392.

8. Saul, John Ralston. 2014. *The Comeback.* Chapter 1. Interesting read on the *righteousness of Canadian policies toward aboriginal peoples. History Is Upon Us.* Pp. 1-14.

9. See: https://www.umanitoba.ca/cm/cmarchive/vol12no3/white-hoods.html: Julian Sher. *White Hoods: Canada's Ku Klux Klan.* Vancouver, New Star Books, c1983.

10. http://www.thecanadianencyclopedia.ca/en/article/orange-order/

11. "The great aim of our legislation has been to do away with the tribal system and assimilate the Indian people in all respects with the other inhabitants of the Dominion as speedily as they are fit to change." Sessional Papers 20B. 1887, Volume 16. Memorandum of John A. MacDonald to the Honourable the Privy Council of Canada.

12. Timothy J. Stanley. *John A. Macdonald's Aryan Canada: Aboriginal Genocide and Chinese Exclusion.* January 2015. Activehistory.ca.

http://activehistory.ca/2015/01/john-a-macdonalds-aryan-canada-aboriginal-genocide-and-chinese-exclusion/

13. John Raston Saul. *Reflections of a Siamese Twin*, Canada at the end of the Twentieth Century. Penguin Books 1998. Pp. 64-65.

14. Dahl, Jens. "From Ethnic to Political Identity." *Nordic Journal of International Law*. 1988. 3: 312-315.

15. Loukacheva, Natalia, *Arctic Promise: Legal and Political Autonomy of Greenland and Nunavut*. University of Toronto Press, 2007 - 266 pages. In Chapter 1: From Subjugation to Self-Government? : In the opinion of Dahl, these were key steps towards political unity and the formation of a true Greenlandic nation, which was in sharp contrast to the fragmentation that characterizes the Inuit of Canada and Alaska. P. 23.

16. ITK. First Canadians, Canadians first. A National Strategy on Inuit Education. 20111. http://www.itk.ca/wp-content/uploads/2011/06/National-Strategy-on-Inuit-Education-2011.pdf

17. In Ross, W. Gillies, *This Distant and Unsurveyed Country, A Woman's Winter at Baffin Island*, 1857-58. McGill-Queen's University Press. Pp 50-51.

18. Taylor, John Leonard, *Canadian Indian Policy During the Inter-War Years, 1918-1939*, Department of Indian Affairs and Northern Development, 1981.

19. Diubaldo, Richard, "The Absurd Little Mouse: When Eskimos Became Indians," *Journal of Canadian Studies*, 16.2 (Summer 1981) Until 1939, there appears to have existed only a limited moral obligation on the part of Ottawa toward the Eskimos; certainly it was not a legal one.

20. See R. Quinn Duffy. *The Road to Nunavut*, Kingston & Montreal. McGill Queen's University Press. 1987. P. 16. The official but careless guardian of the Inuit let the wicked uncle (Editor's note: a.k.a. the Hudson's Bay Company) have his way with them.

21. In 1904, the name changed into Royal North West Mounted Police, until 1920 when amalgamated with the Dominion police, it became the Royal Canadian Mounted Police.

22. See Marjolaine Saint-Pierre, *Joseph-Elzéar Bernier, Champion of Canadian Arctic Sovereignty*, Baraka Books 2009, p. 234.

23. Loukacheva 2007. P. 23.

24. The comments of Diamond Jenness on the administration of the Arctic are enlightening: Eskimo Administration II. Arctic Institute of North America Technical Papers No. 14. Montreal, 1964; P. 25.

25. Keith J. Crowe, *A History of The Original Peoples of Northern Canada.* McGill Queen's University Press. 1974-1991. Page 163.

26. Idem. P. 173.

27. Melanie Gagnon and Iqaluit Elders. *Inuit Recollections on the Military Presence in Iqaluit. Memory and History in Nunavut.* Vol 2. Pp. 9-11.

28. Dave McIntosh. *Unbuttoned.* Stoddart. Ottawa, 1987. P. 134.

29. Duffy 1987. The actual degree of both the neglect and the exploitation became widely known when the Second World War sent American and Canadian military personnel and civilians to the Arctic. P. 16.

30. Amagoalik, John. *Changing the Face of Canada.* 2007. Edited by Louis McComber, Nunavut Arctic College. 2007. See Chapter 1: Relocation to Resolute Bay. P. 15.

31. James William Daschuk. *Clearing the Plains: Disease, Politics of Starvation, and the Loss of Aboriginal Life.* University of Regina Press, 2013.

32. Idem. P. 136.

33. Bryce, Henderson Peter. *The Story of a National Crime.* James Hope and Sons, Limited. Ottawa 1922. P. 3.

34. Crowe 1974-1991: pp. 165-166.

35. Okpik, Abe, *We Call It Survival.* Nunavut Arctic College. Iqaluit, 2005. P. 46.

36. Crowe 1974-1991: P. 110.

37. United Nations. *Convention on the Prevention and Punishment of the Crime of Genocide.* Adopted by the General Assembly of the United Nations on 9 December, 1948. "In the present Convention, genocide means any of the following acts committed with intent to destroy, in whole or in part, a national, ethnical, racial or religious group, as such: (a) Killing members of the group; (b) Causing serious bodily or mental harm to members of the group; (c) Deliberately inflicting on the group conditions of life calculated to bring about its physical destruction in whole or in part; (d) Imposing measures intended to prevent births within the group; (e) Forcibly transferring children of the group to another group." https://treaties.un.org/doc/publication/unts/volume%2078/volume-78-i-1021-english.pdf

38. Bonesteel, Sarah, *Canada's Relationship with Inuit: A History of Policy and Program Development.* Indigenous and Northern Affairs Canada. 2006. P. 72 http://www.aadnc-aandc.gc.ca/DAM/DAM-INTER-HQ/STAGING/texte-text/inuit-book_1100100016901_eng.pdf

39. United Nations. The Universal Declaration of Human Rights. 1948. http://www.un.org/en/universal-declaration-human-rights/

40. http://www.thecanadianencyclopedia.ca/en/article/indian-act/

41. Government of Canada: http://www.aadnc-aandc.gc.ca/eng/1100 100010189/1100100010191

42. *The Canadian Encyclopaedia*: http://www.thecanadianencyclopedia.ca/en/article/calder-case/

43. Nunavut Tunngavik Inc. Nunavut Land Claims Agreement. 1993. Nunavut Political Development http://nlca.tunngavik.com/?page_id=263#ANCHOR264

44. Jens Dahl, Gender Parity in Nunavut? http://arcticcircle.uconn.edu/SEEJ/Nunavut/gender.html

45. Tunisia gets unique gender parity election law: http://kvinfo.org/news-and-background/tunisia-gets-unique-gender-parity-election-law

46. http://www.statcan.gc.ca/daily-quotidien/170327/dq170327c-eng.pdf

47. Jim Bell, Opposition mounts against Keewatin pilot project. *Nunatsiaq News*, May 21, 1998. http://www.nunatsiaqonline.ca/archives/nunavut980531/nvt80522_05.html. Leave "pilot project" to Nunavut. http://www.nunatsiaqonline.ca/archives/back-issues/week/80306.html#12

48. *The Nunavut Act*, Department of Justice Canada. http://laws-lois.justice.gc.ca/eng/acts/N-28.6/

49. Wilkin, Dwane, Anawak: Few Inuit are qualified in professions. *Nunatsiaq News*, November 19, 2018. http://www.nunatsiaqonline.ca/archives/nunavut981130/nvt81120_03.html

50. Jim Bell, Where are the men? *Nunatsiaq News*, May 27, 2005.

51. Norquay, Geoff, "Building a Nation on Permafrost." *Ipolitics*, June 2014. The idea of splitting the Northwest Territories into two territories first emerged in the 1950s when the non-aboriginal population of the Mackenzie Valley argued that the move would hasten the development of responsible government and spur the economy in the western part of the region. Diefenbaker's government actually proposed such legislation in 1963, but it subsequently died on the order paper. http://ipolitics.ca/2014/06/29/building-a-nation-on-permafrost/

52. Med Emerg Report http://pubs.aina.ucalgary.ca/health/66596.pdf

53. Idem.

54. McKenzie, Cameron, "Medevac and Beyond: The Impact of Medical Travel on Nunavut Residents." *Journal of Aboriginal Health*, Summer 2015. P.81.

55. Idem.

56. Vail, Stephen and Graeme Clinton. "Nunavut Economic Outlook," Conference Board of Canada, May 2001.

57. Varga, Peter. "New Iqaluit port aims for more sealift efficiency, safety." *Nunatsiaq News*. Iqaluit March 24, 2017.

58. Idem.

59. *Nunatsiaq News*, "Ottawa settles with Nunavut Inuit, pays $255.5M in compensation", May 04, 2015.

60. Van Rassel, Jason. "Leaders will plan for Nunavut-behind closed doors." *Nunatsiaq News*, May 10, 1996.

61. Bell, Jim. "Nunavut's 1999-2000 budget: $626 million to start with." *Nunatsiaq News*, June 24, 1998.

62. Idem.

63. Bell, Jim. "Can the Dream of Nunavut Be Salvaged?" *Nunatsiaq News*, 1999, October 22. http://www.nunatsiaqonline.ca/archives/ nunavut991030/editorial.html

64. Martin, Ian. "Inuit Language Loss in Nunavut: Analysis, Forecast, and Recommendations." Glendon College, York University March 7, 2017. "Finance Canada Question 10: Are there other items for which the determination of funding levels should be left open-for finalization at a later date?... GNWT: Yes. A number of items have been identified which we know will have costs associated with them, but the size of the cost is currently not known. The requirement to make Inuktitut a working language in Nunavut is one example." Margaret Melhorn, NWT Deputy Minister of Finance, letter to Barbara Anderson, Dept of Finance Canada (Jan. 8, 1998).

65. LeTourneau, Michele. Report favours English education, Northern News Services. Monday, November 23, 2015.

66. Martin. Op. cit. p. 2.

67. *Royal Commission on Aboriginal Peoples*, Volume 3, Gathering Strength, Chapter 4, "Housing". P. 341.

68. Nunavut Housing Corporation. Corporate Business Plan 2000-2001 to 2001-2003. P. 4.

69. Bell, "Jim, Todd: We'll try to cut deficit in one year." *Nunatsiaq News*: February 9, 1996.

70. Bell, Jim, "Knowledge is power, auditor general says." *Nunatsiaq News,* February 8, 2002.

71. *Nunatsiaq News*, April 11, 2003. Big earnings for Northern Property REIT: Northern Property Real Estate Investment Trust, one of northern Canada's largest owners of rental properties, beats its own earn-

ings projections in the last three months of 2002. The company posted net earnings of $2.4 million, or 24¢ a share, for the last quarter of 2002, exceeding its own forecasts by 20 percent. Northern Property, created through a restructuring of a company formerly known as Urbco, owns more than $250 million worth of office and apartment buildings in Nunavut, the Northwest Territories, and Alberta.

72. *Nunatsiaq News,* December 2002: "The Auditor General of Canada says the government of Nunavut is spending too much money on office space and staff housing leases, and should look at owning buildings rather than leasing them."

73. Bell, Jim. "The GNWT and Nunavut." *Nunatsiaq News,* January 17, 1997.

74. Bourgeois, Annette. "Baffin leaders pessimistic about changing Nav Canada fees." July 1998. http://www.nunatsiaqonline.ca/archives/nunavut980731/nvt80717_11.html

75. Bourgeois, Annette. "Food mail subsidy: limited help for high freight rates." August 8, 1997. http://www.nunatsiaqonline.ca/archives/back-issues/week/70808.html#3

Conclusion

1. Pinasuaqtavut, Our Hopes and Plans for Nunavut. Government of Nunavut. 1999.

Bibliography

Amagoalik, J. (2007). *Changing the Face of Canada*. Nunavut Arctic College. Iqaluit. Edited by Louis McComber.

Argetsinger, T. H. A. (2009). "The Nature of Inuit Self-Governance in Nunavut Territory." Senior Honors Thesis for Native American Studies, Dartmouth College Hanover, New Hampshire.

Berger, T. (2006). "Conciliator's Final Report." Craig E. Jones, Counsel to the Conciliator. The Nunavut Project.

Bonesteel, S. (2006). "Canada's Relationship with Inuit: A History of Policy and Program Development." Indigenous and Northern Affairs Canada.

Bryce, H. P. (1922). *The Story of a National Crime*, James Hope & Sons, Limited.

Bulbulian, M. (1987). *Dancing Around the Table*. National Film Board.

Crowe, K. J. (1974-1991). *A History of The Original Peoples of Northern Canada*. McGill Queen's University Press.

Dahl, J. (1988). "From Ethnic to Political Identity." *Nordic Journal of International Law 3*: 312-315.

Daschuk, J. W. (2013). *Clearing the Plains: Disease, Politics of Starvation, and the Loss of Aboriginal Life*. University of Regina Press.

Diubaldo, R. (Summer 1981). " The Absurd Little Mouse: When Eskimos Became Indians." *Journal of Canadian Studies* 16.2.

Duffy, R. Q. (1987). *The Road to Nunavut*. McGill Queen's University Press.

Gagnon, M. and Iqaluit Elders (2002). *Inuit Recollections on the Military Presence in Iqaluit*. Nunavut Arctic College, Memory and History in Nunavut (2): 212.

Harvey, R. (2004). "Une entrevue avec Paul Okalik – Une terre en quête d'appartenance." *Le Devoir*, 12 juin 2004.

Hicks, J. and White, G. (2005). "Building Nunavut Through Decentralization or Carpet-Bombing into Near-Total Dysfunction? A Case Study in Organizational Engineering." Paper presented at the Annual Meeting of the Canadian Political Science Association University of Western Ontario, London, Ontario.

Innis, H. (1999). *The Fur Trade in Canada: An Introduction to Canadian Economic History*. University of Toronto Press.

Jenness, D. (1964). "Eskimo Administration II." Arctic Institute of North America Technical Papers No. 14 (Montreal).

Légaré, A. (2009). "Le Nunavut : entre le rêve et la réalité Bilan de dix années d'autonomie gouvernementale inuite et pro-spective socio-économique." *Journal of Canadian Studies/ Revue d'études canadiennes* 43(2).

Loukacheva, N. (2007). *Arctic Promise: Legal and Political Autonomy of Greenland and Nunavut*. University of Toronto Press.

Martin, I. (2017). "Inuit Language Loss in Nunavut: Analysis, Forecast, and Recommendations " Glendon College, York University

Maurice, E. B., and Millman, L. (2005). *The Last Gentleman Adventurer: Coming of Age in the Arctic*. Houghton Mifflin Harcourt.

McIntosh, D. (1987). *Canada Unbuttoned*. Stoddart. Ottawa.

McKenzie, C. (summer 2015). "Medevac and Beyond: The Impact of Medical Travel on Nunavut Residents." *Journal of Aboriginal Health.*

Müller-Wille, L. (2014). *The Franz Boas Eningma, Inuit, Arctic and Sciences,* Baraka Books.

Müller-Wille, L. and Gieseking, B. (2012). *Inuit and Whalers on Baffin Island through German Eyes, Wilhelm Weike's Arctic Journal and Letters (1883-84),* Baraka Books.

Okpik, A. (2005). *We Call It Survival.* Nunavut Arctic College. Iqaluit. Edited by Louis McComber.

Partners, M. (2002). "Building Nunavut Through Decentralization: Evaluation Report." Evaluation and Statistics Division. Dep't of Executive and Intergovernmental Affairs Government of Nunavut.

Penikett, T. and Goldenberg, A. (2013). "Closing the Citizenship Gap in Canada's North: Indigenous Rights, Arctic Sovereignty, and Devolution in Nunavut." *Michigan State International Law Review* [Vol. 22.1.]

Quassa, P. A. (2008). *We Need to Know Who We Are.* Nunavut Arctic College. Iqaluit. Edited By Louis McComber: 240.

Ross, W. G. (1997). *This Distant and Unsurveyed Country, A Woman's Winter at Baffin Island, 1857-58.* McGill-Queen's University Press.

Royal-Commission-on-Aboriginal-Peoples (2005). *Gathering Strength.* Volume 3 (Chapter 4, "Housing").

Saint-Pierre, M. (2009). *Joseph-Elzéar Bernier, Champion of Canadian Arctic Sovereignty.* Baraka Books.

Saul, J. R. (1998). *Reflections of a Siamese Twin, Canada at the end of the Twentieth Century.* Penguin Books.

Saul, J. R. (2014). *The Comeback.* Viking.

Sher, J. (1983). *White Hoods: Canada's Ku Klux Klan.* New Star Books, Vancouver.

Stanley, T. J. (2015). "John A. Macdonald's Aryan Canada: Aboriginal Genocide and Chinese Exclusion." Active History. ca January 7, 2015.

Tapardjuk, L. (2013). *Fighting for Our Rights*. Nunavut Arctic College. Edited by Jaypeetee Arnakak, Frédéric Laugrand and Louis McComber.

Taylor, J. L. (1981). "Canadian Indian Policy During the Inter-War Years, 1918-1939." Department of Indian Affairs and Northern Development.

Vail, S. and Clinton, G. (2001). *Nunavut Economic Outlook*. The Conference Board of Canada.

White, G. (2009). "Governance in Nunavut: Capacity vs. Culture?" *Journal of Canadian Studies/Revue d'études canadiennes* 43(2).

Zellen, B. S. (2008). *Breaking the Ice: From Land Claims to Tribal Sovereignty in the Arctic*. Lexington Books.

Zellen, B. S. (2009). *On Thin Ice: The Inuit, the State, and the Challenge of Arctic Sovereignty*. Rowman & Littlefield.

Index

MIX
Paper from
responsible sources
FSC® C100212

Printed by Imprimerie Gauvin
eau, Québec